NUTS

NUTS

50 Tasty Recipes, from Crunchy to Creamy and Savory to Sweet

PATRICK EVANS-HYLTON

Photography by Hilary McMullen

SASQUATCH BOOKS
SEATTLE

To my husband, Wayne Hylton, for his complete, unwavering support in all my endeavors.

To my grandmother, Ma'am-Ma (Barbara Evans), who raised me since infancy, for instilling in me at an early age the love of the written word and the craft of cooking.

Printed in China

Published by Sasquatch Books
19 18 17 16 15   9 8 7 6 5 4 3 2 1

Editor: Gary Luke
Production editor: Emma Reh
Photographs: Hilary McMullen
Design: Joyce Hwang
Food styling: Julie Hopper
Copyeditor: Diane Sepanski

Library of Congress Cataloging-in-Publication Data is available.

ISBN: 978-1-63217-021-7

Sasquatch Books
1904 Third Avenue, Suite 710
Seattle, WA 98101
(206) 467-4300
www.sasquatchbooks.com
custserv@sasquatchbooks.com

CONTENTS

RECIPE LIST

ACKNOWLEDGMENTS

Thank you to Gary Luke of Sasquatch Books for the opportunity to work with your wonderful company again. I greatly appreciate the offer to pen *Nuts*.

Also, thank you to Sasquatch Books production editor Emma Reh for great insight and guidance, and to Diane Sepanski for detailed copyediting, Joyce Hwang for gorgeous design, and Hilary McMullen for outstanding photography.

Thank you, too, to my agent, Michael Psaltis of The Culinary Entertainment Agency, for his assistance with this project, for all his guidance, and for his friendship.

And to my family and friends, much appreciation to you for all your support in letting me bounce off ideas and thoughts, and for lending encouragement along the way.

NUTS, IN A NUTSHELL

Nuts are one of the oldest known foods. Prehistoric humans consumed them regularly as part of their diet—seven types of nuts were found at a 780,000-year-old archaeological site in Israel's Hula Valley in 2002.

What were prehistoric humans eating? Among the nuts were almonds and pistachios, and alongside were rudimentary nutcrackers to open them up.

References to other nuts go back centuries. Walnuts were loved by the Romans, who named them *Juglans regia*, or "Jupiter's royal acorn." The Bible references almonds and pistachios as among the "choice fruits of the land" in Genesis 43:11.

Portable and high in protein, nuts went with early travelers and are noted as being must-haves along the 4,000-mile Silk Road, which connected trade between China and other parts of the Asian continent with the West some 2,000 years ago. George Washington loved Brazil nuts and pecans so much that he carried them around in his pockets; John Adams quipped that he cracked them open with his teeth, resulting in the need for dentures (which, by the way, were not wooden). And, following the Civil War, the peanut became America's nut, synonymous with treats at the ballpark and circus. Shortly after this, around the turn of the last century, another one of our favorite treats was invented—peanut butter.

Nuts are such a part of our culinary experience that it's easy to take them for granted. There are classic recipes involving nuts, such as marzipan, pesto, and satay. There are old-school dishes such as trout amandine, and snacks from peanut butter and jelly sandwiches to banana nut bread. It's hard to imagine snacking without a bowl of mixed nuts or a holiday without a nut-laden fruitcake. Modern takes include nut milks and cheeses, part of a vegan or vegetarian diet for many.

But these examples just scratch the surface. There are many types of nuts, and many ways to enjoy them.

NUT VARIETIES

The word *nut* is derived from the Latin *nux*, which references the nutmeat inside the shell. And that is what, by definition, a nut is: edible meat, or a kernel/seed, surrounded by a hard or woody shell. These true nuts are sometimes called tree nuts to differentiate them from other edibles that people call nuts, such as peanuts. The nuts focused on in this book are the most common and accessible nuts:

ALMOND: A drupe, which is the stone or pit surrounding the seed of a fleshy fruit, almonds have their origin in the Middle East; today California is the largest grower. Almonds are eaten raw or toasted, either out of hand or in both savory and sweet dishes. They are also commonly made into almond butter, almond milk, and almond oil, and flavor almond extract and liqueurs such as amaretto.

CASHEW: This nut grows on the end of the cashew apple (or cashew fruit) and is native to Brazil; today Nigeria is the largest grower. Cashew nuts are eaten raw or toasted, either out of hand or in both savory and sweet dishes. Cashews are also often used as a thickening agent in Indian and Southeast Asian soups, stews, and milk-based desserts because of their starch content. They are commonly made into cashew butter and cashew milk.

CHESTNUT: There are several varieties, with cultivation evident from around 2000 BC. Unlike most other nuts, chestnuts are not enjoyed in their raw state due to high levels of tannic acid. They are eaten boiled or roasted, either out of hand or in both savory and sweet dishes. Chestnuts are also often milled into flour. They are a holiday staple as a roasted snack and in stuffing.

HAZELNUT: This nut is also known as a filbert. Hazelnuts are found in savory dishes, but more often in sweets such as truffles, tortes, and the classic French cake, *dacquoise*. Hazelnuts are used to make the liqueur Frangelico and the chocolate spread Nutella. They are eaten raw, boiled, toasted, or roasted, either out of hand or in both savory and sweet dishes. Turkey is a large grower; Oregon is also strongly associated with hazelnuts.

MACADAMIA NUT: Macadamia nuts are native to Australia, although many folks associate them with Hawaii, where they are also grown commercially. They are eaten raw or toasted, either out of hand or in both savory and sweet dishes, but because of their rich, buttery flavor, they are often found in desserts.

PEANUT: This nut is actually a legume that grows on runners underground. A native of South America, it made its way to Africa and came to the United States with the slave trade sometime in the late seventeenth or early eighteenth century. Peanuts can be eaten raw or toasted, either out of hand or

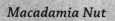

Macadamia Nut

Walnut

Almond

Hazelnut

Pistachio

Cashew

Chestnut

Pine Nut

Pecan

Peanut

in both savory and sweet dishes; many savory dishes are Asian in origin. Peanut butter has been a favorite for more than a hundred years.

PECAN: Native to Mexico and a relative of the hickory, pecans were grown by such founding fathers as George Washington and Thomas Jefferson. They can be eaten raw or toasted, either out of hand or in both savory and sweet dishes. In America, classic pecan sweets include divinity, pecan pie, and fruitcake. Texas is a large pecan-producing state.

PINE NUT: This is not actually a nut, but rather an edible seed from pine trees. All pine nuts are edible, but only some species of pines produce nuts large enough to be worth harvesting. They can be eaten raw or toasted, either out of hand or in both savory and sweet dishes.

PISTACHIO: Native to the Mediterranean, this drupe grows in grapelike clusters. Iran is the largest grower, with California second in pistachio production. The nuts can be eaten raw or toasted, either out of hand or in both savory and sweet dishes. Pistachios are a key element in baklava.

WALNUT: Middle Eastern in origin, walnuts are primarily grown in China and Iran, with California coming in third. The nut can be eaten raw or toasted, either out of hand or in both savory and sweet dishes. Most common is the Persian or English walnut. There is also the black walnut, native to North America. Walnut oil is often used in cooking because of its high smoke point.

> I've also included recipes that incorporate some legumes and seeds that are used culinarily like nuts: pumpkin seeds (pepitas), sesame seeds, and sunflower seeds.

KNOW YOUR NUTS

SELECTING AND STORING NUTS

Nuts are available in many different forms: still in the shell, already shelled, raw, roasted, and brined among them. They are typically sold in bulk bins or already packaged from gourmet, grocery, and health food stores. If you are lucky to visit a nut tree orchard or perhaps a farm stand or farmers' market in the "peanut belt," you might buy some direct from the grower, but generally you don't get to pick and choose the nuts you buy as you would fruits and vegetables.

The nuts you purchase should be just fine, but do check to see if there is a best-by date on the package, or, if you are able, find out when the nuts were harvested. Nuts are perishable—they can go stale, which makes them unpleasant to eat. They can also go rancid, which could make them unhealthy to eat. The best rule of thumb is that if the nut smells or tastes off, or has an unusual texture, throw it out. Smell and sample nuts before use.

Here are a few things to keep in mind once you get your nuts home:

- Store nuts in a sealable glass or plastic container; do not use metallic containers.
- Nuts easily pick up strong aromas; make sure the container you store them in is airtight.
- Nuts should be stored out of direct sunlight.
- Storing nuts in a cool, dark place will keep them fresh for up to three months, depending on the nut.
- Refrigerating nuts extends their use up to six months; nuts can be used right out of the refrigerator.
- Freezing nuts extends their use up to one year; allow nuts to sit at room temperature for about five minutes before use.
- Label nut containers with the date to keep on top of how fresh they are.
- Nuts that are unsalted will store longer than salted nuts.
- Whole nuts will store longer than chopped nuts.
- Nuts in the shell will store longer than shelled nuts.
- Nuts that are still usable but slightly stale can be toasted to make them more palatable.
- Once a nut has become soft or soggy, it needs to be tossed.
- Seeds such as pine nuts, pumpkin seeds, sesame seeds, and sunflower seeds will keep only about a third as long as tree nuts and drupes.

PREPARING NUTS

It pays to buy your nuts raw and whole. Packaged nuts that have already been roasted and/or chopped cost significantly more; you are paying a convenience fee for something you could do rather easily and quickly yourself.

Here's how to prepare your nuts the way you want them:

BUTTER: Nut butters are made by processing a nut, usually in a food processor, until it is spreadable. Peanut butter is the most typical nut butter, but almond and cashew butters are common as well. See Peanut Butter (page 27).

CHOP: Sometimes you need chopped nuts, whether for use in baked goods or sprinkling on top a dish as a garnish. Nuts can be chopped to varying cuts, from finely chopped to roughly chopped, depending on their use.

An 8-inch chef's knife, or similar, is best for chopping smaller amounts of nuts. Place the nuts on a steady cutting surface, grasp the handle, and place your other hand on the top center of the knife blade while you rock it back and forth over the nuts, keeping the knife tip on the cutting board.

A food processor is also good to chop nuts, especially in larger quantities, but pulse it several times rather than letting the blade run. Keep an eye on the processing so the nuts do not get pureed into a butter.

Always roast/toast nuts before chopping.

MILK: Nut milk is made by processing a nut, usually in a food processor, along with water and sometimes a sweetener, then straining the mixture so a liquid is the final product. Almond milk is the most typical nut milk. See Almond Milk (page 31).

ROAST/TOAST: Nuts that are roasted impart a more crisp texture, golden color, and smoky, toasted flavor. Nuts can be roasted in the oven or toasted in a sauté pan or skillet on the stove. Some people have had success using microwave ovens, but the nuts don't brown and their textures can be off. See Techniques for Roasting and Toasting Nuts (page 11).

SOAK: Soaking nuts and seeds makes them softer and easier to use in certain applications; this is especially good when processing or blending. Nuts are soaked before processing into nut milk. You can also soak nuts to reduce any dust or residue from the surface or release any thin, papery skin from the outside. Some say soaking increases the nut's nutrients and makes them easier to digest.

Nuts are soaked anywhere from a half hour to overnight; typically, the larger and harder the nut, the longer the soak. Check nuts after 20 minutes; if they yield a bit when squeezed, they are close to being ready. At this point, you should also change out the soaking water; it will brown and become murky the longer the nuts sit in it.

If you soak nuts for any use other than blending or processing, you can dry them and crisp them back up in a food dehydrator or slow oven.

NUT-RITIONAL ASPECTS

Nuts are a nutrient-dense food; most pack in a good amount of dietary fiber, minerals, and vitamins. Among the minerals present in many nuts are copper, iron, magnesium, manganese, phosphorus, selenium, and zinc. Vitamins include the B vitamins folate, niacin, pantothenic acid, pyridoxine, riboflavin, and thiamine, and vitamin E. And while nuts do contain a good amount of oil, which means they are higher in fat, these are the good monounsaturated and polyunsaturated fats.

Nuts are cholesterol-free, and nuts in their basic form are gluten-free; some packaged nuts may have additives that introduce a gluten product, so check the label.

TECHNIQUES FOR ROASTING & TOASTING NUTS

Roasting and toasting time can vary due to several factors, such as the size of nuts, size of pan, and type of heat (oven or stovetop) applied. Because of their oil content, nuts and seeds can burn quickly—always watch them closely in the last few minutes of roasting or toasting.

Be sure to use raw nuts or seeds, not ones that have already been cooked or processed in some other way.

Adding a bit of oil results in crispness when roasting and toasting, and you can use any complimentary oil in place of the neutral canola I suggest, but nuts can be dry-roasted, too. To dry-roast nuts, simply omit the oil in the recipe, but take caution to make sure the nuts' own oil does not scorch during the process.

ROASTING AND BOILING CHESTNUTS

An American classic, the chestnut has a bit of romanticism about it, especially during the holidays. Use peeled chestnuts right away, or store them in a sealed container in the refrigerator for about two weeks. Peeled chestnuts can also be placed in a freezer bag and frozen for about three months.

Roasting Chestnuts

MAKES 2 DOZEN

- Preheat the oven to 350 degrees F. Soak **2 dozen chestnuts** in warm water for about 30 minutes to soften their hard shells. Dry them well so they won't be slippery when you cut them.
- With a sharp knife, cut an X on the bottom (flat) side of the chestnut through the shell and just into the flesh. The X should be from about the middle of the nut across.
- Put the chestnuts on a rimmed baking pan. Roast until the cut shell peels back to expose the meat inside, 30 to 35 minutes. While the chestnuts are still warm, but cool enough to safely handle, remove and discard the shell and the papery skin around the flesh.

Boiling Chestnuts

MAKES 2 DOZEN

- Soak **2 dozen chestnuts** in warm water for about 30 minutes to soften their hard shells. Dry them well so they won't be slippery when you cut them.
- With a sharp knife, cut an X on the bottom (flat) side of the chestnut through the shell and just into the flesh. The X should be from about the middle of the nut across.
- In a large stockpot, bring water to a boil and add the prepared chestnuts. Cook the chestnuts until they are tender and soft when squeezed, about 15 minutes, then drain the water. While the chestnuts are still warm, but

cool enough to safely handle, remove and discard the shell and the papery skin around the flesh.

ROASTING PEANUTS IN THE SHELL

Peanuts roasted in the shell make a delicious snack. You can also shell the roasted nuts to use in recipes or process into Peanut Butter (page 27). To roast shelled peanuts, see Roasting and Toasting Tree Nuts (page 16).

MAKES 1 POUND

- Preheat the oven to 350 degrees F. Rinse off **1 pound raw peanuts in the shell** and pat them dry. In a large bowl, stir them together with **1 tablespoon canola oil** and **2 tablespoons sea salt**.
- Transfer the peanuts to a rimmed baking sheet and bake, stirring every 5 to 7 minutes and watching to make sure they do not burn, until the shells begin to brown, about 25 to 35 minutes. Let cool before shelling.

ROASTING AND TOASTING PINE NUTS

Pine nuts, called *pinoli* in Italian (often spelled "pignoli" in the United States) are found in many of that country's best-known dishes, such as pesto and *biscotti ai pinoli*. The salt can be omitted, or other seasonings can be used in its place or in addition to it—from savory (cayenne pepper, chili powder, or dried herbs) to sweet (cinnamon sugar, ginger, or nutmeg).

Roasting Pine Nuts

MAKES 1 CUP

- Preheat the oven to 350 degrees F. In a small bowl, stir together **1 cup raw pine nuts, 1 tablespoon canola oil,** and **1 teaspoon sea salt**.

- Transfer the pine nuts to a rimmed baking sheet and bake, stirring once or twice and watching to make sure they do not burn, until golden brown, about 5 to 10 minutes. Let cool before eating.

Toasting Pine Nuts

MAKES 1 CUP

- In a medium sauté pan, heat **2 tablespoons canola oil** over medium heat.
- Add **1 cup raw pine nuts** and stir constantly until they begin to become fragrant and golden brown, about 3 to 5 minutes, making sure they do not burn.
- Remove the pine nuts with a slotted spoon to a bowl, add **1 teaspoon sea salt**, and toss to cover. Drain on paper towels. Let cool before eating.

ROASTING AND TOASTING PUMPKIN SEEDS

Pumpkin seeds are used very much like a nut, for snacking or in recipes from baked goods to granola. They are a good substitute for sunflower seeds in many recipes, and you can use these recipes to roast and toast sunflower seeds as well.

The salt can be omitted, or other seasonings can be used in its place, or in addition to it—from savory (cayenne pepper, chili powder, or dried herbs) to sweet (cinnamon sugar, ginger, or nutmeg).

Roasting Pumpkin Seeds

MAKES 1 CUP

- Preheat the oven to 325 degrees F. In a small bowl, stir together **1 cup raw pumpkin seeds**, **1 tablespoon canola oil**, and **1 teaspoon sea salt**.
- Transfer the seeds to a rimmed baking sheet and bake, stirring every 5 to 7 minutes and watching to make sure they do not burn, until golden brown, about 25 to 35 minutes. Let cool before eating.

Toasting Pumpkin Seeds

MAKES 1 CUP

- In a medium sauté pan, heat **2 tablespoons canola oil** over medium heat.
- Add **1 cup raw pumpkin seeds** and stir constantly until they begin to become fragrant and golden brown, about 4 to 7 minutes, making sure they do not burn.
- Remove the seeds with a slotted spoon to a bowl, add **1 teaspoon sea salt**, and toss to cover. Drain on paper towels. Let cool before eating.

ROASTING AND TOASTING SESAME SEEDS

Sesame seeds are the edible seeds of the flowering sesame plant, and just a few seeds impart a lot of nutty flavor. Because the seeds are very small and have a high oil content, it is not necessary to add additional oil during the roasting or toasting process. As they are an ingredient and not eaten out of hand, no seasoning is used.

Roasting Sesame Seeds

MAKES ½ CUP

- Preheat the oven to 325 degrees F.
- Evenly distribute **½ cup raw sesame seeds** across a rimmed baking sheet and bake, stirring once or twice and watching to make sure the seeds do not burn, until golden brown, about 5 to 10 minutes. Let cool before using.

Toasting Sesame Seeds

MAKES ½ CUP

- In a medium sauté pan over medium heat, add **½ cup raw sesame seeds** and stir constantly until they begin to become fragrant and golden brown, about 3 to 5 minutes, making sure they do not burn. Let cool before using.

ROASTING AND TOASTING TREE NUTS

Roasting and toasting nuts adds extra crunch and brings out essential oils. Use these recipes to roast and toast shelled peanuts as well as tree nuts, such as almonds, cashews, hazelnuts, macadamia nuts, pecans, pistachios, and walnuts. The salt can be omitted, or other seasonings can be used in its place, or in addition to it—from savory (cayenne pepper, chili powder, or dried herbs) to sweet (cinnamon sugar, ginger, or nutmeg).

Roasting Tree Nuts

MAKES 1 CUP

- Preheat the oven to 350 degrees F. In a small bowl, stir together **1 cup raw nuts**, **1 tablespoon canola oil**, and **1 teaspoon sea salt**.
- Transfer the nuts to a rimmed baking sheet and bake, stirring every few minutes and watching to make sure they do not burn, until golden brown, about 8 to 12 minutes. Let cool before eating.

Toasting Tree Nuts

MAKES 1 CUP

- In a medium sauté pan, heat **2 tablespoons canola oil** over medium heat.
- Add **1 cup raw nuts** and stir constantly until they begin to become fragrant and golden brown, about 5 to 7 minutes, making sure they do not burn.
- Remove the nuts with a slotted spoon to a bowl, add **1 teaspoon sea salt**, and toss to cover.
- Drain on paper towels. Let cool before eating.

ROASTING IN THE MICROWAVE

Tree nuts and shelled peanuts can be roasted in a microwave, but I have found mixed results. It can, at times, lead to uneven roasting and texture and color that is a bit off, so I typically recommend just roasting them in a skillet on the stovetop.

If you do roast your nuts in a microwave, here are some tips:

- The nuts do not have to be tossed in oil, but if you want to do so and sprinkle on some salt or other flavoring, that is fine.
- As with traditional methods, if chopped nuts is your desired finished product, roast nuts whole and then chop.
- Spread nuts evenly out on a microwave-safe plate.
- Like melting chocolate in a microwave, roasting nuts should be done in intervals. Do not place the nuts in the microwave, set it, and walk away.
- If you have a cup or fewer of nuts, microwave on high for 2 minutes, then look at the nuts, stir them, microwave for 1 minute more, and repeat. Pick up one of your nuts and bite it. If it doesn't have a firm, crisp texture and pleasant toasted flavor, roast again at 1-minute intervals, up to 5 to 8 minutes total, until you reach the desired taste and texture.
- Roasting time varies a bit by the microwave, type of nut, and size of the nut.
- Remember that when roasting nuts—whether in the microwave, on the stovetop, or in the oven—the nuts continue to cook a bit even once removed from the heat, so adjust accordingly.

A NOTE ON TOASTING

Often times whether to toast nuts or leave them raw before adding them to a recipe is entirely up to personal preference. For recipes that do not specify raw or toasted nuts, either will work.

SPICE
BLENDS

A spicy Louisiana bayou-inspired blend, this fiery mix of hot smoked paprika with earthy herbs and spices will make your taste buds sit up and take notice.

BAYOU BOOGALOO

MAKES ABOUT 1 CUP

¼ cup hot smoked paprika

¼ cup ground cumin

¼ cup ground coriander

2 tablespoons dried oregano

1 tablespoon garlic powder

1 tablespoon freshly ground
    black pepper

1 tablespoon coarse
    kosher salt

2 teaspoons cayenne pepper

- In a large bowl, whisk together all the ingredients. Transfer to an airtight container and store in a cool, dark place for up to 6 months.
- To serve, mix 2 to 3 tablespoons of the spice blend with 1 cup of nuts, preferably just after roasting or toasting.

This blend is reminiscent of the spices used in fall-centric pies like pumpkin and sweet potato. The demerara sugar adds a hint of sweetness.

AWESOME AUTUMN

MAKES ABOUT 1 CUP

½ cup ground cinnamon

¼ cup demerara sugar

4 teaspoons ground ginger

4 teaspoons ground nutmeg

4 teaspoons ground allspice

2 teaspoons ground cloves

- In a large bowl, whisk together all the ingredients. Transfer to an airtight container and store in a cool, dark place for up to 6 months.
- To serve, mix 2 to 3 tablespoons of the spice blend with 1 cup of nuts, preferably just after roasting or toasting.

Rich, earthy Indian-esque flavors abound in this blend.

CURRY IN A HURRY

- In a large bowl, whisk together all the ingredients. Transfer to an airtight container and store in a cool, dark place for up to 6 months.
- To serve, mix 2 to 3 tablespoons of the spice blend with 1 cup of nuts, preferably just after roasting or toasting.

MAKES ABOUT 1 CUP

¼ cup ground cumin

¼ cup ground coriander

¼ cup ground turmeric

1 tablespoon ground cardamom

1 teaspoon ground cloves

1 teaspoon ground cinnamon

1 teaspoon cayenne pepper

1 teaspoon kosher salt

1 teaspoon freshly ground black pepper

This dry mix's classic down-home taste makes it perfect for simple social gatherings, such as a tasting of craft beers or barbecues and cookouts. The flavor is slightly piquant and a bit earthy.

DOWN ON THE RANCH

MAKES ABOUT 1 CUP

½ cup dried parsley

2 tablespoons dried dill

2 tablespoons garlic powder

2 tablespoons onion powder

1 teaspoon dried thyme

1 teaspoon dried basil

1 teaspoon coarse
kosher salt

1 teaspoon freshly ground
black pepper

- In a large bowl, whisk together all the ingredients. Transfer to an airtight container and store in a cool, dark place for up to 6 months.
- To serve, mix 2 to 3 tablespoons of the spice blend with 1 cup of nuts, preferably just after roasting or toasting.

Fiery pepper elements mix with the complex flavors of the unsweetened cocoa in this blend that honors the Mexican sauce, mole.

MOLE OLÉ!

- In a large bowl, whisk together all the ingredients. Transfer to an airtight container and store in a cool, dark place for up to 6 months.
- To serve, mix 2 to 3 tablespoons of the spice blend with 1 cup of nuts, preferably just after roasting or toasting.

MAKES ABOUT 1 CUP

½ cup chili powder

4 teaspoons ground cumin

4 teaspoons ground coriander

4 teaspoons smoked paprika

4 teaspoons sweet paprika

4 teaspoons unsweetened cocoa powder

2 teaspoons garlic powder

2 teaspoons coarse kosher salt

1 teaspoon cayenne pepper

1 teaspoon crushed red pepper flakes

1 teaspoon freshly ground black pepper

STAPLES

Peanut Butter 27

Mushroom-Walnut Sauce 28

Hazelnut-Bourbon-Chocolate Sauce 29

Almond Milk 31

Green Olive–Pistachio Tapenade 32

Pig-Mento & Pecan Cheese 33

Walnut Compote 34

Peanut butter, a spread consisting of roasted peanuts ground into a paste, can be traced back to Aztec times, but modern peanut butter goes back to 1884 for a patent for a peanut product that had "a consistency like that of butter, lard or ointment."

Making your own peanut butter is quick and easy, plus the result is fresh and you can control (and pronounce) all the ingredients that go into it. Other nut butters, including almond, cashew, and walnut butter, are made in a similar fashion.

For honey-roasted peanut butter, add 2 teaspoons of honey after you begin to pulse to break the peanuts up, just before adding the salt.

PEANUT BUTTER

- Put the peanuts in the bowl of a food processor fitted with the steel blade attachment and drizzle 2 tablespoons of the oil over the top. Pulse to break up the peanuts, add the salt and sugar, and blend until very smooth. (For a chunky version, stop before the peanut butter reaches a smooth consistency.) Scrape down the sides periodically. If the mix is very dry, drizzle in more oil by the teaspoonful. Store the peanut butter in an airtight container in the refrigerator for up to 2 months.

MAKES APPROXIMATELY 3½ CUPS

4 cups roasted, unsalted Virginia peanuts

2 to 3 tablespoons vegetable or peanut oil

1 teaspoon kosher salt

1 teaspoon sugar (optional)

Virginia produces several varieties of peanuts, including Spanish and Valencia, but it became well known for its namesake Virginia peanut, which has a large, rich, buttery kernel.

This sauce is full of umami, the taste element that describes earthy, savory components. Mushrooms, walnuts, and the merlot's tannins mesh to create a rich, simple sauce great for spooning over grilled or roasted beef, chicken, or pork dishes, or a big helping of mashed potatoes.

MUSHROOM-WALNUT SAUCE

MAKES ABOUT 1 CUP

4 tablespoons (½ stick) unsalted butter, divided

6 cloves garlic, minced

4 pounds fresh mushrooms, sliced

2 tablespoons freshly squeezed lemon juice

2 cups merlot

½ cup toasted walnuts, chopped

¼ cup chopped flat-leaf parsley

1 teaspoon coarse sea salt

½ teaspoon freshly ground black pepper

• In a large sauté pan over medium heat, melt 1 tablespoon of the butter, then add the garlic. Stir and add the mushrooms. Continue to stir until the mushrooms start to brown and soften, about 5 to 10 minutes. Stir in the lemon juice. Reduce the heat to low and add the wine. Simmer, stirring occasionally, until the wine reduces by about half, 10 to 15 minutes. Remove the pan from the heat. Stir in the remaining 3 tablespoons butter until it has melted, then stir in the walnuts, parsley, salt, and pepper.

The walnut tree doesn't start producing until it is around fifteen years old; the average tree produces for about forty-five years.

Hazelnuts have a true affinity with chocolate, as this rich, buttery sauce shows. Quick and easy to prepare, the sauce gets another subtle layer of flavor from the small addition of bourbon, without it being overpowering as in a typical hard sauce. Drizzle it over cakes, cookies, brownies, and, of course, a big bowl of ice cream.

HAZELNUT-BOURBON-CHOCOLATE SAUCE

- In a heavy saucepan over medium heat, heat the cream and milk. Add the butter, stirring until it melts, and then bring the mixture to a gentle, rolling boil. Place the chocolate in a stainless steel or glass bowl and pour the cream mixture over the top. Allow to stand for 5 minutes and stir until smooth. Stir in the bourbon and hazelnuts, and serve immediately or store in an airtight container in the refrigerator for up to 3 days.

MAKES ABOUT 1 CUP

½ cup heavy cream

¾ cup milk

2 tablespoons (¼ stick) unsalted butter

½ pound dark chocolate, chopped into ¼-inch pieces

2 tablespoons bourbon

¼ cup toasted, chopped hazelnuts

Hazelnuts are also known as filberts, which may be a tribute to St. Philibert's Day on August 22, around when filberts ripen in England, or a derivative of "full beard," referencing the husk or beard covering the nut in certain varieties.

Almond milk is one hot commodity in the grocery store, but it's easy to make at home. The best part is you control the quality of the ingredients. Use it like you would regular milk: to drink, on cereal, in smoothies and shakes, and the like. Cashew and walnut milk are made in the same manner. Make sure to use raw nuts.

ALMOND MILK

- Put the almonds in a bowl and cover them with water. Cover the bowl, and let the almonds soak overnight to soften them for easier blending.
- Drain the almonds and add them to a blender with the water. Pulse to break the almonds up, then blend on high for 2 to 3 minutes, stopping if needed to scrape down the sides of the blender. Blend until the almonds are as smooth as you can get them, then add 2½ cups of water, the honey, vanilla, and salt, and blend on high for 2 to 3 minutes.
- Line a strainer with cheesecloth and place it over a large bowl. Pour the almond mixture into the strainer, scraping out all the bits from the blender. Pull up the corners of the cheesecloth, twist the top closed, and squeeze the cloth with your hands to extract as much of the milk as you can. You can freeze the leftover ground almonds for use in baking.
- Taste and add more honey, if needed. Store the almond milk in an airtight container in the refrigerator for 2 to 3 days.

MAKES APPROXIMATELY 4 CUPS

1½ cups raw almonds

1½ cups water

1½ teaspoons honey or maple syrup

1 teaspoon vanilla extract

¼ teaspoon kosher salt

There are more than thirty varieties of almonds.

This is an updated take on the classic olive spread, which is typically made with black olives or a mix of black and green olives. This tapenade uses green ones, as well as that favorite green nut, the pistachio. Use it as a sandwich spread, a topping for bruschetta, spooned over fish or chicken, stuffed in an omelet, or any other way you would use a traditional tapenade.

GREEN OLIVE–PISTACHIO TAPENADE

MAKES ABOUT 1 CUP

½ cup pistachios, toasted

½ cup assorted green olives, pitted

2 tablespoons capers

2 tablespoons flat-leaf parsley leaves (no stems)

1 clove garlic, roughly chopped

1 tablespoon freshly squeezed lemon juice

1 teaspoon lemon zest

½ teaspoon freshly ground black pepper

2 to 3 tablespoons extra-virgin olive oil

• In a blender, pulse the pistachios, olives, capers, parsley, garlic, lemon juice, lemon zest, and pepper until roughly chopped. Drizzle in the oil, 1 tablespoon at a time, and pulse until the mixture comes together in a chunky-textured paste. Store the tapenade in an airtight container in the refrigerator for up to 5 days.

Recipes featuring pistachios were included in *Apicius*, a first-century Roman cookbook.

Tangy, sassy pimento cheese gets kicked up a notch with the addition of smoky bacon and toasty pecans in this ever-so-satisfying update of a classic. This spread is great on celery ribs, slathered on hamburgers, added to a cheese plate, or dolloped on a baked potato. Or shape it into a ball and roll it in additional pecans for a take on the classic cheese ball.

PIG-MENTO & PECAN CHEESE

MAKES ABOUT 3 CUPS

- In a large bowl, combine the cheeses, bell pepper, and onion. In a medium bowl, whisk together the mayonnaise, vinegar, salt, celery seed, black pepper, and cayenne. Pour the mayonnaise over the cheese mixture, mix well, and taste, adjusting the mayonnaise and seasonings for texture and flavor. Fold in the bacon and pecans. Refrigerate for at least 2 hours before serving.

1 cup shredded sharp cheddar cheese

1 cup shredded mild cheddar cheese

1 roasted red bell pepper, cored, seeded, and chopped

½ small sweet onion (such as Vidalia), finely chopped

½ cup mayonnaise

2 tablespoons apple cider vinegar

½ teaspoon kosher salt

½ teaspoon celery seed

¼ teaspoon freshly ground black pepper

¼ teaspoon cayenne pepper

6 to 8 slices crisply cooked bacon, chopped

½ cup toasted pecans, chopped

> Pecan trees can live—and bear edible nuts—for more than three hundred years.

This compote is a great addition to a cheese board, especially paired with stronger cheeses like blues. Toasty elements from the pan-roasted walnuts come together with the sweetness of dates, cherries, and honey and are accented with just a hint of salt and pepper. It also makes a wonderful topping for roasted chicken or pork, turkey burgers, or as a filling in buckwheat crepes.

WALNUT COMPOTE

MAKES ABOUT 1 CUP

1 tablespoon unsalted butter

½ cup raw walnuts, coarsely chopped

6 dates, pitted and coarsely chopped

½ cup dried cherries

¼ cup water

2 tablespoons honey

½ teaspoon kosher salt

¼ teaspoon freshly ground black pepper

- In a medium sauté pan, melt the butter over medium-high heat. Add the walnuts and toast, stirring occasionally, until they begin to brown and turn fragrant, about 3 to 4 minutes. Reduce the heat to medium-low and add the dates, cherries, water, honey, salt, and pepper. Simmer, stirring occasionally, until the liquid reduces and the compote comes together, about 5 to 7 minutes. Store the compote in an airtight container in the refrigerator for 3 to 4 days.

The California walnut is a descendent of the Persian walnut, where the tree is native.

SNACKS

This is a treat that many folks make for gatherings and gift-giving at the holidays, but it is delicious for snacking year-round; chop the nuts to top ice-cream sundaes or ambrosia, or toss in a salad—especially one with pears or strawberries—for a sweet, crunchy touch. You can also substitute walnuts for the pecans.

CANDIED PECANS

- Preheat the oven to 250 degrees F. Grease a rimmed baking sheet and set it aside.
- In a mixing bowl, beat the egg white, vanilla, and water just until soft peaks begin to appear; the mixture will be frothy. In a separate bowl, combine the sugar, salt, cinnamon, and nutmeg. Add the pecans to the egg-white mixture, tossing to coat. Transfer the nuts to the sugar mixture and toss to coat. Spread the nuts out evenly on the baking sheet.
- Bake at 250 degrees F for 1 hour, stirring every 10 to 15 minutes. Watch the nuts in the last 15 to 20 minutes of cooking for doneness: the nuts will be golden brown and firm, and the sugar coating will have hardened. Store the pecans in an airtight container in a cool, dry place for up to 2 weeks.

MAKES 1 CUP

1 egg white

½ tablespoon vanilla extract

½ tablespoon water

1 cup sugar

¾ teaspoon kosher salt

½ teaspoon ground cinnamon

¼ teaspoon ground nutmeg

1 pound raw pecan halves

CAYENNE CANDIED PECANS

Follow the recipe above. When combining the sugar, salt, cinnamon, and nutmeg, added a dash of cayenne pepper to the dry ingredients. Proceed with the recipe as written.

This popcorn treat goes well beyond the traditional offering of melted butter and salt as toppings. I took four favorite nuts, paired them with salty popcorn, candied the mix, and made it even more delightful by dipping it in melted chocolate.

NUTTY POPCORN MUNCH

MAKES 4 TO 6 SERVINGS

4 quarts freshly popped corn

¼ cup pecan halves

¼ cup walnut halves

¼ cup hazelnuts

¼ cup macadamia nuts

1 cup packed dark
   brown sugar

½ cup dark corn syrup

½ cup (1 stick) unsalted
   butter

½ teaspoon kosher salt

½ teaspoon baking soda

1 teaspoon vanilla extract

2 cups milk chocolate chips

- Preheat the oven to 250 degrees F. Line a rimmed baking sheet with aluminum foil or a silicone baking sheet and set it aside. Put the popcorn in a large bowl. In a medium bowl, combine the pecans, walnuts, hazelnuts, and macadamia nuts.

- In a heavy 2-quart saucepan over medium heat, add the brown sugar, corn syrup, butter, and salt. Stir constantly until the mixture reaches a boil, then allow it to boil for 5 minutes without stirring. Remove the pan from the heat and stir in the baking soda and vanilla.

- Pour the sugar mixture over the popcorn, add the nut mixture, and toss to combine. Spread the popcorn mixture evenly over the prepared baking sheet and bake for 45 minutes, stirring occasionally. Remove the baking sheet from the oven and allow the popcorn to cool. Break the mixture into medium-size pieces.

- Using a double boiler, melt the chocolate chips. For instructions on how to melt chocolate in a double boiler or how to create your own double boiler, see Using a Double Boiler (note follows).

- Line another baking sheet with aluminum foil or a silicone baking sheet. Dip each piece of the popcorn mixture into the chocolate to coat on all sides. Place the pieces on the baking sheet and let the chocolate harden, about 15 minutes, before serving.

USING A DOUBLE BOILER

To melt chocolate in a double boiler, add a few inches of water to the bottom pan, making sure the water does not touch the top pan. Remove the top pan, put the chocolate in it, and set aside. Over medium-low heat, bring the water to a simmer, reduce the heat to low, and place the top pan back on the bottom pan. Let the chocolate soften, and turn off the heat.

As the chocolate begins to melt, stir it gently with a plastic spatula. Just before all the chocolate has melted, remove the top pan and set it on the counter, stirring until all the chocolate is melted and smooth.

DIY DOUBLE BOILER

To improvise a double boiler, use a metal or glass bowl sitting firmly on top of a saucepan and follow the instructions above.

Although folks have been eating treats in the great outdoors since time immemorial, the making of the modern-day trail mix is claimed by two California growers who mixed up an energy snack of peanuts and raisins in the late 1960s. This mix pays homage with a tasty blend of nuts and fruits that you'd find growing in California, with an extra bonus of some white chocolate chip morsels.

CALIFORNIA DREAMIN' TRAIL MIX

- In a large bowl, combine all the ingredients. Transfer to an airtight glass container and store in a cool, dry place for up to 1 month.

MAKES 5 CUPS

1 cup almonds

1 cup pistachios

1 cup walnuts

½ cup dates, chopped

½ cup dried figs, chopped

½ cup golden raisins

½ cup white chocolate chips

Boiled peanuts are a true Southern delicacy, with the brine of seaside oysters and the texture of edamame. Most of the time boiled peanuts are eaten plain as a snack, but you can craft dishes using the soft legume inside; for example, they make a delicious hummus, replacing the traditional chickpeas. Be sure to use raw, green peanuts in the shell for this recipe and not ones that have already been cooked or processed in some other way.

SOUTHERN-STYLE BOILED PEANUTS

MAKES 4 POUNDS

4 pounds raw peanuts in
the shell

4 cups salt

- Rinse the peanuts under cold running water, drain, and put them in a large stockpot with the salt. Add enough water to cover the peanuts. Bring the water to a rapid boil, then reduce to a simmer, stirring occasionally, for approximately 4 hours, or until the peanuts are dark and moist. Add additional water if needed to keep the peanuts covered.
- Remove one or two peanuts and crack them open. Taste for texture and flavor; the peanuts should be soft and salty. If the peanuts still have a crunch to them, continue cooking, checking every 15 minutes until done.

- Remove the peanuts from the heat. If they are at the desired saltiness, drain them immediately. If they are not salty enough, allow them to cool in the brine, which allows more salt to be absorbed. Check periodically for salt levels. Leftovers can be stored in an airtight container in the refrigerator for up to 10 days.

More than two-thirds of all snack nuts eaten in the United States are peanuts, making them the nation's number one snack nut.

Most likely born out of not letting a good thing go to waste, banana bread uses those ripe bananas that may otherwise be discarded and turns them into a homey pleasure for brunch, breakfast, dessert, snacks, and gift-giving. This version is enhanced with the distinctive taste of macadamia nuts and a simple glaze atop.

MACADAMIA NUT BANANA BREAD

- To make the bread, preheat the oven to 325 degrees F. Grease a 9-by-5-inch loaf pan and set it aside.
- In a large bowl, beat together the eggs, buttermilk, and oil. Stir in the bananas. In a separate bowl, whisk together the sugars, flour, baking soda, salt, and cinnamon. Gradually add the dry ingredients to the wet ingredients, stirring with each addition. Stir in the macadamia nuts. Pour the batter into the loaf pan and use a spatula to even out the top. Bake until the top is golden and a toothpick inserted in the center comes out clean, 75 to 85 minutes.
- Cool the bread in the pan for about 15 minutes, then finish cooling it on a wire rack.
- While the bread cools, make the glaze. In a large bowl, whisk together the confectioners' sugar, almond extract, and 2 tablespoons of the cream until smooth. Add the additional tablespoon of cream if needed to thin the glaze. When the bread has cooled, drizzle the glaze over it.

MAKES 1 LOAF

FOR THE BREAD:

2 eggs

⅓ cup buttermilk

½ cup canola oil

1 cup mashed bananas (about 3 medium bananas)

1 cup granulated sugar

½ cup packed dark brown sugar

1¾ cups all-purpose flour

1 teaspoon baking soda

½ teaspoon kosher salt

½ teaspoon ground cinnamon

½ cup chopped macadamia nuts

FOR THE GLAZE:

1 cup confectioners' sugar

½ teaspoon almond extract

2 to 3 tablespoons heavy cream

The 1950s classic cocktail peanut mix, updated. Gone may be the days of the two-martini lunch, but folks still want a good nut mix to enjoy while having a drink or two. Cayenne Candied Pecans bring a little heat and a little sweet for a delicious snack.

PISTACHIO-WASABI COCKTAIL NUT MIX

MAKES 5 CUPS

1½ cups salted peanuts

1 cup pistachios

1 cup Cayenne Candied Pecans (page 39)

½ cup miniature pretzels

½ cup wasabi peas

½ cup small, thin wheat crackers

- In a large bowl, combine all the ingredients. Transfer to an airtight container and store in a cool, dry place for up to 1 month.

CHOCOLATY PISTACHIO WASABI NUT MIX

2 cups Pistachio-Wasabi Cocktail Nut Mix or other salty nut-based snack mix

2 cups white chocolate chips

- Put the nut mix in a ziplock bag and gently crush it into smaller pieces. Line a baking sheet with parchment paper and set it aside.
- Using a double boiler, melt the chocolate chips. For instructions on how to melt chocolate in a double boiler or how to create your own double boiler, see Using a Double Boiler (page 41).
- Pour the nut mix in a large bowl with the melted chocolate and stir to completely coat. Drop by the rounded teaspoonful onto the prepared baking sheet. Put the baking sheet, uncovered, in the freezer until the chocolate is firm, about 20 minutes.

Filled with favorite nut varieties, Gold-Standard Granola satisfies with a few unique offerings too: pine nuts, pumpkin seeds, and the subtle flavors of maple and cinnamon. Eat it for breakfast or as a snack, or use it to top ice cream or Greek yogurt drizzled with honey. For a variation, add a cup of chocolate chips at the same time you add the dried cranberries and raisins.

GOLD-STANDARD GRANOLA

- Preheat the oven to 250 degrees F. Lightly grease two rimmed baking sheets and set them aside.
- In a large bowl, toss together the oats, coconut, almonds, cashews, walnuts, pine nuts, and pumpkin seeds. In a separate bowl, combine the brown sugar, maple syrup, oil, honey, salt, and cinnamon. Pour the mixture over the dry ingredients and toss to coat. Pour the granola evenly onto the prepared baking sheets and spread it out. Bake the granola for 75 minutes, stirring it every 10 to 15 minutes. Let it cool for 10 minutes. Transfer the granola to a large bowl and toss it with the cranberries and raisins. Store granola in an airtight container at room temperature for up to 5 days.

> Pumpkin seeds are used culinarily like nuts. Their Spanish name is *pepitas de calabaza* meaning "little seeds of squash."

MAKES 8 CUPS

2½ cups rolled oats

½ cup shredded coconut

½ cup raw slivered almonds

½ cup raw chopped cashews

½ cup raw chopped walnuts

¼ cup pine nuts

¼ cup Toasted Pumpkin Seeds (page 15)

¼ cup packed dark brown sugar

¼ cup maple syrup

¼ cup canola oil

2 tablespoons honey

¾ teaspoon kosher salt

½ teaspoon ground cinnamon

1 cup dried cranberries

1 cup golden raisins

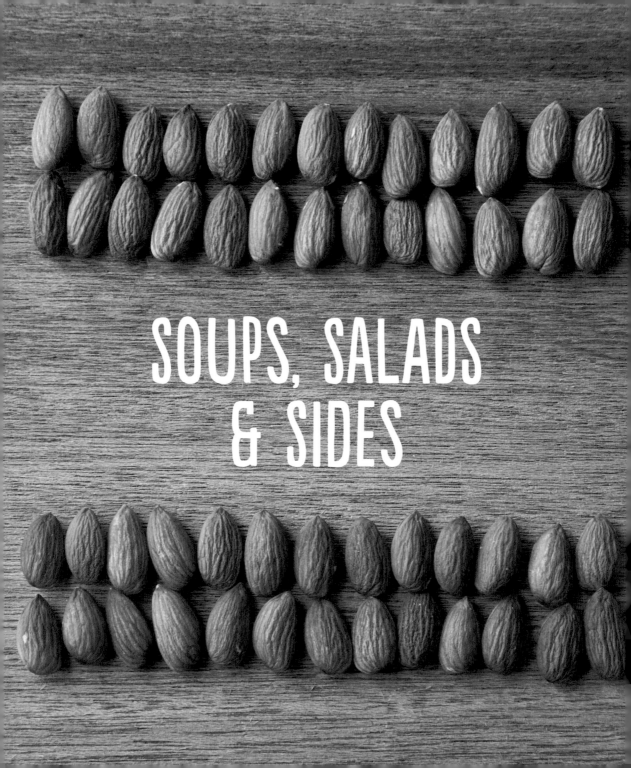

SOUPS, SALADS & SIDES

Rich, creamy peanut butter is the base for this surprisingly savory soup, which you are likely to find all across Colonial Williamsburg and in many fine-dining restaurants in Virginia, such as the Regency Room at the Hotel Roanoke.

WILLIAMSBURG PEANUT SOUP

MAKES 8 SERVINGS

- In a large saucepan over medium heat, cook the celery and onion until the vegetables have softened and are turning translucent, 3 to 5 minutes. Add the butter and continue cooking until the vegetables are translucent, about 5 minutes (do not brown the butter). Add the flour, and stir until blended. Add the chicken broth and bring the soup to a boil. Reduce the heat to medium and cook, stirring occasionally, until the soup reduces slightly, about 15 minutes.
- Pour the soup through a sieve into a large bowl, pressing hard against the solids with the back of a spoon. Discard the solids, return the liquid to the saucepan, and heat on medium-low. Add the peanut butter and cream, and stir constantly until blended. Add the pepper. Heat for 5 minutes, stirring constantly.
- To serve, divide the soup among 8 bowls. Garnish with the peanuts and thyme, and serve immediately.

2 celery stalks,
  finely chopped

1 medium sweet onion
  (such as Vidalia),
  finely chopped

¼ cup (½ stick) unsalted
  butter

3 tablespoons all-purpose
  flour

2 quarts (8 cups) chicken
  stock

2 cups smooth Peanut
  Butter (page 27) or
  store-bought

1¾ cups light cream

½ teaspoon freshly ground
  white pepper

Virginia peanuts, finely
  chopped, for garnish

Fresh thyme sprigs,
  for garnish

It wasn't until 1842 that Dr. Matthew Harris planted the first commercial peanut crop in Waverly, Virginia, near the town of Wakefield, where the Virginia Diner today is noted for their peanuts.

This delicious, creamy soup is perfect in the autumn or winter. I like to serve it garnished with cornbread croutons, but you could also add some crispy, thinly sliced ham or chopped, cooked chorizo on top.

CREAMY CHESTNUT SOUP WITH CORNBREAD CROUTONS

MAKES 4 TO 6 SERVINGS

FOR THE CROUTONS:

3 to 4 tablespoons unsalted butter, melted

1 (8-by-8-inch) pan day-old cornbread, cut in ½-inch cubes

1 to 2 teaspoons bay-flavored seafood seasoning

FOR THE SOUP:

2 pounds roasted or boiled chestnuts, shelled and halved

1 quart (4 cups) chicken stock

½ teaspoon cayenne pepper

½ teaspoon freshly ground white pepper

½ teaspoon kosher salt

½ teaspoon freshly grated nutmeg

2 teaspoons fresh thyme leaves

1 cup heavy cream

2 tablespoons chopped flat-leaf parsley, for garnish

- To make the croutons, preheat the oven to 400 degrees F. On a baking sheet, drizzle the butter over the cornbread and lightly toss to coat. Sprinkle on the bay seasoning (or salt and pepper) and lightly toss to coat.
- Bake for 10 to 15 minutes, or until the cornbread crisps and turns golden, turning halfway through. Remove from the oven and set aside to cool.
- To make the soup, in a large stockpot over medium heat, cook the chestnuts and stock for about 20 minutes, stirring occasionally, until heated and the chestnuts have softened.
- Blend the soup until smooth, using an immersion blender, or in batches in a blender or food processor fitted with a steel blade attachment. Return the soup to the stockpot and heat on medium.
- Add the cayenne, pepper, salt, nutmeg, and thyme, and stir to incorporate. Simmer the soup for 5 minutes.
- Stir in the cream and simmer for an additional 5 to 10 minutes, or until heated. Do not allow the soup to come to a boil or the cream may curdle.
- Garnish with the croutons and parsley and serve immediately.

The refreshing flavors of watermelon and tender butter lettuce—also known as butterhead, bibb, or Boston lettuce—get a bit of a punch from some salty, pungent feta cheese and toasty, earthy pine nuts in this salad that is a great composition of taste and texture.

WATERMELON, FETA & TOASTED PINE NUT SALAD WITH CHAMPAGNE VINAIGRETTE

- To make the dressing, in a medium bowl, whisk together all the ingredients and set aside.
- In a large bowl, drizzle 4 tablespoons of the dressing on the lettuce and toss to coat.
- To serve, divide the salad among 4 plates, and top with the watermelon, cheese, and pine nuts. Drizzle lightly with additional dressing.

About 20 species of pines produce seeds large enough for harvesting; they have been gathered for food since the Paleolithic period.

MAKES 4 SERVINGS

FOR THE DRESSING:

¼ cup extra-virgin olive oil

2 tablespoons champagne vinegar

½ teaspoon sea salt

¼ teaspoon freshly ground black pepper

FOR THE SALAD:

4 cups butter lettuce, torn

4 cups seedless watermelon, cubed

⅓ pound feta cheese, crumbled

¼ cup toasted pine nuts

Perfectly chilled steamed shrimp, with a clean taste of premium Japanese beer and lemon, meet a sweet-hot sauce over noodles studded with fresh vegetables in this Asian-inspired treat. You can make the shrimp and noodles ahead of time, and quickly whip up the dressing and toss it with the vegetables and sesame seeds for an easy work-night dinner.

CHILLED SHRIMP & PASTA SALAD WITH FIERY PEANUT BUTTER DRESSING

- To prepare the shrimp and pasta, in a medium saucepan over medium-high heat, bring the beer and water to a boil. Add the lemon peel and shrimp. Cover and steam the shrimp until they are firm and have turned pink, 2 to 3 minutes. Drain through a sieve, discarding the lemon peel, then run the shrimp under cold water, draining well. Transfer the shrimp to a covered bowl and refrigerate for at least 1 hour.

- Meanwhile, bring 4 quarts of salted water to a boil in a large stockpot over medium-high heat. Add the pasta, and cook, stirring frequently, until the pasta is al dente, 7 to 10 minutes. Drain through a sieve, then run the pasta under cold water; place the sieve over the sink and let the pasta drain completely. Transfer the pasta to a covered bowl and refrigerate for at least 1 hour.

- To make the dressing, in a large bowl, whisk together all the ingredients. Set aside.

(continued)

MAKES 4 TO 6 SERVINGS

FOR THE SHRIMP AND PASTA:

½ cup Japanese beer (such as Sapporo or Kirin Ichiban)

½ cup water

Peel of 1 large lemon

1 pound large shrimp, peeled and deveined

½ pound whole wheat linguine

FOR THE DRESSING:

¼ cup creamy Peanut Butter (page 27) or store-bought

1½ tablespoons soy sauce

1½ tablespoons rice vinegar

1 tablespoon honey

1 teaspoon sesame oil

1½ teaspoons grated peeled ginger

1 clove garlic, minced

½ teaspoon crushed red pepper flakes

¼ teaspoon freshly ground black pepper

FOR THE SALAD:

1½ tablespoons black sesame seeds

1½ tablespoons white sesame seeds

1 cup fresh edamame, shelled (or frozen and thawed)

1 red bell pepper, cored, seeded, and cut into small dice

1 large carrot, coarsely shredded

1 small bunch scallions, green and white parts, thinly sliced

- To make the salad, in a large frying pan over medium heat, toast the sesame seeds, shaking the pan occasionally to move them around, until the seeds begin to brown and turn fragrant, about 3 to 5 minutes. Set aside. Add the dressing to the pasta and toss well to coat. Add the edamame, bell pepper, carrots, and scallions. Gently toss.
- To serve, put the shrimp on top of the dressed noodles and sprinkle with the toasted sesame seeds.

Originally consumed primarily by the poor and used as feed for livestock, the lowly "goober pea," from an African word for peanut, didn't gain popularity until the Civil War, when it was seen as a portable, compact source of protein.

It seems that just about everyone loves bacon. This salad not only calls for crispy, crumbled bacon on top, but also mixes those delicious bacon drippings into a hot dressing that wilts the sharp-flavored greens, making the perfect platform for crisp, tart apples and crunchy, buttery pecans.

APPLE, BACON & PECAN SALAD WITH HOT BACON DRESSING

- In a large bowl, combine the greens. In a separate bowl, toss the apples in the lemon juice and set aside.
- To make the dressing, in a large skillet over medium-high heat, cook the bacon until crisp. Using a slotted spoon, transfer the bacon to a paper towel–lined plate and set aside.
- Add the onion to the skillet and cook in the bacon fat, stirring occasionally, for about 2 minutes, or until translucent. Add the garlic, stir for 15 seconds, and remove the skillet from the heat. Add the vinegar, and scrape down the sides of the skillet. Stir in the mustard, pepper, salt, and sugar.
- Crumble the reserved bacon and toss the greens in the dressing. To serve, divide the salad among 4 plates, and top with the apples, bacon, and pecans.

MAKES 4 SERVINGS

FOR THE SALAD:

2 cups escarole

2 cups friseé

2 medium Granny Smith apples, peeled, cored, and cut into ¼-inch wedges

1 tablespoon freshly squeezed lemon juice

I cup toasted pecans

FOR THE DRESSING:

6 slices thick-cut bacon, chopped

1 tablespoon finely chopped sweet onion (such as Vidalia)

1 clove garlic, finely minced

¼ cup apple cider vinegar

1 tablespoon Dijon mustard

½ teaspoon freshly ground black pepper

¼ teaspoon kosher salt

¼ teaspoon sugar

Delicate arugula, with its peppery tastes muted, works well with the sweetness of pears in this salad, simply dressed in a vinaigrette with the subtle taste of champagne vinegar throughout. Charming little kisses of goat cheese enrobed in hazelnuts are an added touch.

PEAR & BABY ARUGULA SALAD WITH HAZELNUT–GOAT CHEESE KISSES

- To make the kisses, in a medium bowl, combine the cheese and thyme. Refrigerate until firm, about 1 hour. When the cheese has chilled, using a small melon baller, scoop out balls of cheese and roll them in the hazelnuts. Place them on a baking sheet and refrigerate while preparing the salad and dressing.
- To make the dressing, in a small bowl, whisk together all the ingredients. Set aside.
- To make the salad, in a medium bowl, toss the arugula with the dressing. Divide the salad among 4 or 6 plates, top with the pears, place 1 or 2 kisses on the side, and garnish with the thyme and hazelnuts.

MAKES 4 TO 6 SERVINGS

FOR THE KISSES:

6 ounces creamy goat cheese

1 teaspoon fresh thyme leaves

3 tablespoons toasted hazelnuts, finely chopped

FOR THE DRESSING:

¼ cup extra-virgin olive oil

2 tablespoons champagne vinegar

1 tablespoon Dijon mustard

1 tablespoon honey

½ teaspoon kosher salt

¼ teaspoon freshly ground black pepper

FOR THE SALAD:

5 cups baby arugula

2 pears, thinly sliced

Fresh thyme leaves, for garnish

Coarsely chopped hazel-nuts, for garnish

When beets are roasted their mineral-laden flavor mellows and a rich robustness shines. In this salad, that earthy flavor is met with piquant, creamy gorgonzola and crunchy walnuts, accented by a bright citrus vinaigrette.

BEET, GORGONZOLA & TOASTED WALNUT SALAD

MAKES 4 SERVINGS

FOR THE BEETS:

1½ pounds small red beets, trimmed

1½ pounds small yellow beets, trimmed

6 tablespoons extra-virgin olive oil

1 teaspoon kosher salt

FOR THE DRESSING:

½ cup freshly squeezed orange juice

¼ cup freshly squeezed lemon juice

¼ cup extra-virgin olive oil

1 teaspoon Dijon mustard

½ teaspoon kosher salt

⅛ teaspoon freshly ground black pepper

FOR THE SALAD:

4 cups baby spinach

¼ pound gorgonzola cheese, crumbled

⅓ cup toasted, chopped walnuts

- Preheat oven to 375 degrees F.
- To prepare the beets, place the beets on a foil-lined baking sheet and toss with the oil to coat. Cover with another sheet of foil, and crimp the edges of both pieces to seal. Roast for 25 to 35 minutes, or until a knife can be easily inserted into the beets. Roast longer if needed, checking for doneness every 10 minutes. Remove the beets from the oven and set aside to cool.
- Meanwhile, make the dressing. In a large lidded jar, combine all the ingredients. Shake until well mixed and refrigerate until ready to use. Shake again just before serving.
- When the beets are cool enough to handle, remove the skin with your fingers or a paring knife. Cut them into ¼-inch cubes, sprinkle with the salt, and set aside.
- In a medium bowl, drizzle 4 tablespoons of the dressing on the spinach and toss to coat.
- To serve, divide the salad among 4 plates and top with the beets, cheese, and walnuts. Drizzle lightly with additional dressing.

I updated my ambrosia—a favorite side dish or dessert of the Deep South—a bit by adding some tartness to the dressing's slightly sweetened whipped cream. The pistachios add a rich flavor and a crunch to complement the host of traditional fruit toss-ins.

AMBROSIA FRUIT SALAD WITH PISTACHIOS

- To make the dressing, in a medium bowl using an electric mixer, whip the cream and sugar until stiff peaks form, about 8 minutes. Fold in the sour cream.
- In a large bowl, add the marshmallows, pineapple, orange, coconut, pistachios, and cherries and toss to combine. Add the dressing and toss to incorporate. Cover and refrigerate 2 hours.
- Serve in individual glass bowls garnished with a bit of nutmeg.

MAKES 4 TO 6 SERVINGS

FOR THE DRESSING:

1 cup heavy cream

1 tablespoon confectioners' sugar

½ cup sour cream

FOR THE SALAD:

3 cups miniature marshmallows

1 cup fresh pineapple chunks, or 1 cup from 1 (20-ounce) can, drained

1 cup fresh mandarin orange segments, or 1 cup from (15-ounce) can, drained

1 cup grated coconut

1 cup toasted pistachios

½ cup drained maraschino cherries

Freshly grated nutmeg, for garnish

Roasting and sautéing brussels sprouts brings out elements of this cabbage family relative's natural sweetness, here contrasted by the bite of onion and garlic. Earthy notes from the hazelnuts and salty elements from country ham round out this side dish. Walnuts are an excellent substitute for hazelnuts in this recipe.

PAN-SEARED BRUSSELS SPROUTS WITH HAZELNUTS & FRAZZLED COUNTRY HAM

- In a large sauté pan, heat 1 teaspoon of the oil over medium heat. When the oil is hot, add the ham, and cook, stirring to prevent burning, until crispy, 2 to 3 minutes. Drain the ham on paper towels.
- In a large sauté pan, melt the butter and heat the remaining 2 tablespoons oil over medium heat. Add the brussels sprouts and onion, and cook, stirring occasionally, until the brussels sprouts begin to turn brown and the onion becomes translucent, about 3 minutes. Add the garlic and cook for 1 minute more. Add the broth, thyme, and pepper and bring to a boil. Reduce the heat to low, cover, and simmer until the broth is reduced and the brussels sprouts are fork-tender, about 10 minutes.
- To serve, sprinkle the brussels sprouts with the ham, hazelnuts, and thyme.

MAKES 4 TO 6 SERVINGS

2 tablespoons plus 1 teaspoon extra-virgin olive oil, divided

4 thin slices country-cured ham, sliced into matchsticks

1 tablespoon unsalted butter

1½ pounds brussels sprouts, halved lengthwise

¼ cup chopped white onion

2 cloves garlic, minced

1 cup vegetable broth

1 teaspoon fresh thyme leaves

⅛ teaspoon freshly ground black pepper

½ cup toasted hazelnuts, coarsely chopped

Thyme sprigs, for garnish

This take on chestnut stuffing is richly moist and decadent. It is a perfect side dish to a holiday dinner or any table set for a fine feast. Serve it alongside roasted or grilled pork or poultry.

HERBED CHESTNUT BREAD PUDDING WITH PARMESAN CREAM SAUCE

MAKES 6 TO 8 SERVINGS

FOR THE BREAD PUDDING:

1½ cups (3 sticks) unsalted butter, cubed

2 tablespoons extra-virgin olive oil

2 cups roasted or boiled chestnuts, shelled and chopped

½ small white onion, diced

1 clove garlic, minced

2 tablespoons minced fresh sage leaves

2 tablespoons minced fresh flat-leaf parsley

2 tablespoons fresh thyme leaves

1 tablespoon minced fresh rosemary

1 tablespoon minced fresh basil

- Preheat the oven to 350 degrees F.
- To make the bread pudding, in a sauté pan over medium heat, heat the butter and oil until the butter melts. Add the chestnuts, onion, and garlic, and sauté for 3 minutes, or until the chestnuts and onions soften and the garlic starts turning golden. Add the sage, parsley, thyme, rosemary, basil, salt, black pepper, and pepper flakes and sauté for an additional 2 minutes. Transfer to a medium baking dish. Add the bread and toss to coat. Spread the mixture out evenly in the dish.
- In a small bowl, whisk together the eggs and milk and pour evenly over the bread mixture. Bake for 30 to 45 minutes, or until surface of the pudding rises slightly and turns golden brown.

- To make the sauce, in a sauté pan over medium heat, heat the butter and oil until the butter melts. Add the onion and garlic and sauté for 3 to 5 minutes, or until soft and translucent. Stir in the cream and then the cheese. Reduce the heat to medium-low and stir constantly until the mixture thickens, about 3 to 5 minutes. Stir in the pepper flakes and white pepper. Remove from the heat and add the parsley. Pour the sauce over the pudding and serve immediately.

Chestnuts are often part of the New Year's menu in Japan, symbolizing mastery and strength.

1 teaspoon kosher salt

¼ teaspoon freshly ground black pepper

¼ teaspoon crushed red pepper flakes

6 cups cubed day-old bread

3 eggs

¼ cup milk

FOR THE SAUCE:

¼ cup (½ stick) unsalted butter, cubed

2 tablespoons extra-virgin olive oil

½ small white onion, finely chopped

2 cloves garlic, minced

⅓ cup heavy cream

¼ cup finely grated Parmesan cheese

⅛ teaspoon crushed red pepper flakes

⅛ teaspoon freshly ground white pepper

2 tablespoons chopped flat-leaf parsley

MEAT & POULTRY

Although originating in South America, peanuts have become integral to many Asian cuisines, adding richness to an assortment of dishes. Served over cooling coconut rice, this spicy peanut sauce with seasoned chicken is a satisfying combination.

GRILLED PEANUT CHICKEN SKEWERS OVER THAI COCONUT RICE

- To prepare the chicken, in a medium bowl, whisk together the oil, soy sauce, sugar, garlic, ginger, coriander, pepper flakes, and black pepper. Place the chicken strips in a shallow baking dish and pour the marinade over them. Refrigerate for 2 to 3 hours, turning once.
- About 30 minutes before you want to cook the chicken, make the rice. To make the rice, in a large saucepan, bring the coconut water, coconut milk, salt, and cinnamon stick to a boil. Add the rice, stir, cover the saucepan, and reduce the heat to a simmer. Cook for about 15 minutes, or until the liquid is absorbed. Turn off the heat and let the rice sit, covered, for an additional 15 minutes.
- While the rice cooks, make the peanut sauce. To make the peanut sauce, combine all the ingredients in a blender and process until smooth, about 30 seconds. Set aside.

(continued)

MAKES 4 TO 6 SERVINGS

FOR THE CHICKEN:

2 cups peanut oil

2 tablespoons soy sauce

2 tablespoons dark brown sugar

2 cloves garlic, minced

1 tablespoon minced fresh ginger

1 teaspoon ground coriander

½ teaspoon red pepper flakes

⅛ teaspoon freshly ground black pepper

1 pound boneless, skinless chicken breasts, cut into ½-inch strips

FOR THE RICE:

1½ cups coconut water

1 cup unsweetened coconut milk

1 teaspoon kosher salt

1 cinnamon stick, broken
  in half

2 cups jasmine rice

3 scallions, trimmed and
  chopped

FOR THE SAUCE:

⅓ cup evaporated milk

⅓ cup unsweetened
  coconut milk

⅓ cup smooth Peanut
  Butter (page 27) or
  store-bought

1 tablespoon soy sauce

¼ teaspoon ground ginger

Dash of Asian hot sauce
  (such as sriracha)

FOR THE GARNISH:

1 small bunch cilantro,
  roughly chopped

- Heat a gas or charcoal grill to medium-high and thread the chicken strips on metal or soaked wooden skewers. You'll need 4 to 6 skewers, depending on how the chicken is sliced. (Alternatively, use a grill pan or skillet to cook the chicken indoors.) Grill, turning the skewers every 4 to 5 minutes, until the juices run clear, 12 to 15 minutes.

- To serve, transfer the rice to a serving platter, remove and discard the cinnamon sticks, and sprinkle the scallions over the rice. Arrange the chicken skewers atop the rice, and drizzle the peanut sauce over everything. Garnish with the cilantro.

Romesco is a classic Spanish sauce that sometimes gets overlooked in the United States. Akin to pesto, this rich and hearty sauce is made with roasted tomatoes; in this recipe, a trio of nuts adds greater complexity. Paired with chicken here, it is also good with a number of seafood dishes, vegetables, and lamb, but in Spain, it is used as a dip for charred spring onions. This dish would be great served over Spanish or yellow rice. Any leftover sauce can be stored in an airtight container in the refrigerator for three to four days.

CHICKEN WITH ROMESCO SAUCE

- To make the sauce, in a food processor fitted with a steel blade attachment, pulse the tomatoes, garlic, bread, hazelnuts, almonds, pine nuts, peppers, vinegar, 2 tablespoons of the oil, the salt, paprika, and pepper until the sauce is well mixed and mostly smooth but still has a few chunks. Add additional oil, about a teaspoon at a time, if needed.
- To prepare the chicken, season both sides of each breast with the salt and pepper. In a saucepan over medium heat, add enough oil to cover the bottom of pan and heat to a low simmer. Carefully add the

(continued)

MAKES 4 SERVINGS

FOR THE ROMESCO SAUCE:

1 recipe Roasted Tomatoes (recipe follows)

2 cloves garlic

2 slices toasted crusty bread, torn

⅓ cup toasted hazelnuts

⅓ cup toasted almonds

⅓ cup toasted pine nuts

1 (7.25-ounce) jar roasted red peppers, drained

2 tablespoons red wine vinegar

⅓ cup extra-virgin olive oil

1 teaspoon kosher salt

½ teaspoon smoked paprika

½ teaspoon freshly ground black pepper

4 boneless, skinless chicken breasts

2 teaspoons coarse sea salt

1 teaspoon freshly ground black pepper

2 to 3 tablespoons extra-virgin olive oil

**MAKES ABOUT
2 TO 3 CUPS**

3 large plum tomatoes, halved lengthwise, cored, and seeded

¼ cup extra-virgin olive oil

1 clove garlic, minced

1 teaspoon sugar

1 teaspoon kosher salt

½ teaspoon freshly ground black pepper

chicken breasts. Do not overcrowd the pan. Cook the chicken until it is golden on the bottom and releases easily with tongs, 6 to 8 minutes, depending on thickness. Turn and cook the other side for 5 to 7 minutes. A meat thermometer placed in the thickest part of the breast should read 160 to 165 degrees F and the juices should run clear.

- Spoon the sauce over the chicken and serve.

ROASTED TOMATOES

- Preheat the oven to 450 degrees F.
- Put the tomatoes on a rimmed baking sheet cut side up. Drizzle the oil over them and sprinkle them with the garlic, sugar, salt, and pepper. Roast until the tomatoes begin to reduce and caramelize, 25 to 30 minutes.

The almond has been an important part of Spanish cookery for centuries. Franciscan monks from Spain planted the first almond trees in 1769 as they established missions in California.

First created in the 1890s at the Waldorf Hotel in New York, this fresh, crisp salad quickly became a classic. I add some protein in the form of shredded chicken (roast your own or buy a precooked rotisserie bird at the grocery store) and serve it sans the lettuce in a toasted split-top bun, lobster roll–style. Substituting turkey for the chicken is a great way to use up holiday leftovers.

CHICKEN WALDORF SALAD ROLL

- To make the dressing, in a medium bowl, whisk together all the ingredients and set aside. To make the salad, in a large bowl, combine the chicken, celery, grapes, walnuts, cranberries, raisins, and apple. Pour the dressing over the salad and gently toss to coat. Divide the salad among the rolls and serve.

Walnuts have been eaten by humans for millennia; references go back some nine thousand years.

MAKES 4 SANDWICHES

FOR THE DRESSING:

¾ cup Greek yogurt

¼ cup mayonnaise

1 tablespoon freshly squeezed lemon juice

1 teaspoon orange zest

¼ teaspoon kosher salt

¼ teaspoon freshly ground black pepper

FOR THE SALAD:

2 cups shredded roasted chicken

1 stalk celery, chopped

1 cup seedless red grapes, halved

½ cup toasted walnuts, chopped

¼ cup dried cranberries

¼ cup golden raisins

1 medium Granny Smith apple, cored and chopped (but not peeled)

4 split-top rolls, toasted

Gremolata is a classic chopped herb sauce that is akin to pesto and chimichurri. This version is enriched with the addition of pistachios, which complement the flavor profile of the condiment. You often find gremolata served with osso buco; here it's paired with some simply grilled lamb chops.

LAMB CHOPS WITH PISTACHIO GREMOLATA

- To make the gremolata, in a medium bowl, combine the parsley, pistachios, lemon zest, garlic, salt, and pepper. Drizzle on the oil and gently toss to incorporate. Set aside.
- To prepare the lamb chops, season both sides of the chops with the salt and pepper. Add the oil to a grill pan and heat it over high heat. When the oil is hot, put the chops in the grill pan; do not overcrowd the pan. Sear them on one side for about 2 minutes. Turn the chops over and cook them for an additional 3 minutes.
- Serve each chop topped with about 1 tablespoon of the gremolata.

MAKES 6 SERVINGS

FOR THE GREMOLATA:

¼ cup chopped flat-leaf parsley

2 tablespoons finely chopped toasted pistachios

2 teaspoons lemon zest

1 clove garlic, minced

⅛ teaspoon coarse sea salt

⅛ teaspoon freshly ground black pepper

2 tablespoons extra-virgin olive oil

FOR THE LAMB CHOPS:

6 lamb chops, about ¾ inch thick

2 teaspoons coarse sea salt

1 teaspoon freshly ground black pepper

2 tablespoons extra-virgin olive oil

Pork has a true affinity with rich and sweet flavors, and these chops are in hog heaven encrusted in buttery pecans and accented with bourbon, maple syrup, and even more nuts. This dish would be great served with mashed sweet potatoes and light, fluffy biscuits to sop up all the wonderful tastes.

PECAN-ENCRUSTED PORK CHOPS WITH BOURBON-MAPLE-PECAN BUTTER

MAKES 6 SERVINGS

FOR THE COMPOUND BUTTER:

5 tablespoons unsalted butter, softened

1 tablespoon light brown sugar

1 tablespoon bourbon

1 tablespoon maple syrup

½ cup toasted pecans, finely chopped

FOR THE PORK CHOPS:

1 cup toasted bread crumbs

½ cup toasted pecans, very finely chopped

6 boneless pork chops, ¾ inch thick

2 tablespoons all-purpose flour

1 egg, beaten

- To make the compound butter, in a small bowl, thoroughly combine the butter and brown sugar. Stir in the bourbon and maple syrup, and fold in the pecans. Shape the butter into a log with wax paper, rolling tightly, and refrigerate for at least 2 hours.

- To prepare the pork chops, heat the oven to 400 degrees F. In a bowl, combine the bread crumbs and pecans. Spread them evenly on a plate. Sprinkle both sides of each pork chop with the flour, dip in the egg, and dredge both sides in the bread crumb mixture, evenly coating the chop.

- Place the pork chops on a baking sheet and bake for about 20 minutes; a meat thermometer placed in the thickest part of the chop should read 145 to 150 degrees F, and the juices should run clear.

- Serve each chop with medallions of the butter on top.

Two hallmark flavors of Thanksgiving, turkey and cranberries, come together in this rich burger, sweetened just a bit with dried cherries to offset the cranberries' tartness and given some texture and nuttiness from the addition of walnuts.

THANKSGIVING BURGER

- Preheat a gas grill to high.
- In a large bowl, thoroughly combine the turkey, walnuts, cranberries, cherries, Worcestershire sauce, sage, and pepper. Form ½-inch-thick patties and put them on the grill over direct heat. Grill the patties until a crust forms, 4 to 6 minutes. Flip the patties and grill for an additional 3 to 5 minutes; a meat thermometer placed in the burgers should read 160 to 165 degrees F.
- To serve, top each burger with Brie and place it on a bun with the lettuce and mustard.

MAKES 4 BURGERS

1¼ pounds ground turkey

½ cup toasted walnuts, finely chopped

¼ cup dried cranberries, finely chopped

¼ cup dried cherries, finely chopped

1 teaspoon Worcestershire sauce

½ teaspoon dried ground sage

⅛ teaspoon freshly ground black pepper

FOR SERVING:

Thinly sliced Brie

4 toasted hamburger buns

Butter lettuce

Dijon mustard

One of America's most enduring sandwiches is perhaps the grilled cheese, and while we never outgrow the classic, made with sliced American cheese, this version stretches our taste buds with the decidedly adult flavors of cherries, walnuts, Brie, and bacon. Store any remaining compote in a covered container in the refrigerator for three to four days.

GROWN-UP GRILLED CHEESE WITH CHERRY-WALNUT COMPOTE, BACON & BRIE

- In a small bowl, combine the cherries, jam, and Grand Marnier. Set the compote aside.
- Heat a sauté pan over medium-high heat. Butter one side of each bread slice. Lay 2 slices of bread, butter side down in the pan. Place 2 slices of bacon on each slice. Layer half the Brie and half the goat cheese on top. Fold the walnuts into the compote, and spread a generous spoonful onto the sandwich. Season to taste with salt and pepper. Top each sandwich with the remaining slices of bread, buttered side up.
- Grill the sandwiches until the bread is golden and the cheese has melted, 2 to 4 minutes per side. Serve each sandwich sliced and dusted lightly with the sugar.

MAKES 2 SANDWICHES

½ cup dried cherries, chopped

¼ cup black cherry jam

1 tablespoon Grand Marnier

Unsalted butter, for grilling

4 slices sourdough bread

4 slices bacon, cooked crisp

2 ounces Brie, sliced

2 ounces goat cheese, at room temperature

¼ cup toasted walnuts, finely chopped

Coarse sea salt, for seasoning

Freshly ground black pepper, for seasoning

Confectioners' sugar, for serving

SEAFOOD

Sesame-Coated Seared Tuna over
Wheat Berry–Pistachio Salad 85

Onolicious Tuna Poke Lettuce Cups 87

Parmesan-Crusted Flounder
with Zesto Pesto 88

Pan-Seared Scallops with Orange-Pistachio
Butter over Tagliatelle Pasta 91

Oysters Virginia 93

Since tuna is best when barely cooked, it's imperative to pick the freshest fish possible. In this dish, a light coating of sesame seeds accents the tuna, which is lightly seared and served atop a salad with complementary tangy citrus notes. For a lighter meal, omit the salad and serve the tuna atop fresh, dressed greens, such as arugula or frisée, sprinkled with chopped pistachios.

SESAME-COATED SEARED TUNA OVER WHEAT BERRY–PISTACHIO SALAD

- To make the salad, in a large stockpot, bring 4 quarts of water to a boil over medium-high heat, add the wheat berries, stir, and cook, uncovered, until tender, anywhere from 55 to 65 minutes. Drain the wheat berries through a sieve, running them under cold water. Let the wheat berries drain completely over a sink while making the dressing.
- In a large lidded jar, combine the orange juice, lemon juice, oil, mustard, salt, and pepper. Shake until well mixed.
- Transfer the drained wheat berries to a large bowl and drizzle on the dressing. Add the orange segments, cilantro, and pistachios, and toss to incorporate. Set the salad aside.
- To prepare the tuna, in a bowl, combine the black and white sesame seeds. Spread them evenly on a plate. Sprinkle both sides of the tuna with the salt and pepper and dredge both sides in the sesame seeds, evenly coating the tuna.

(continued)

MAKES 4 SERVINGS

FOR THE SALAD:

2 cups hard winter wheat berries

¼ cup freshly squeezed orange juice (from 1 medium orange)

2 tablespoons freshly squeezed lemon juice

2 tablespoons extra-virgin olive oil

½ teaspoon Dijon mustard

¼ teaspoon kosher salt

¼ teaspoon freshly ground black pepper

1 orange, segmented, connective membrane removed and segments halved

½ cup chopped cilantro

½ cup chopped pistachios

1 cup raw black
    sesame seeds

2 cups white sesame seeds

1 (20-ounce) tuna steak,
    about 1 inch thick

2 teaspoons coarse sea salt

1 teaspoon freshly ground
    black pepper

1 tablespoon butter

3 tablespoons extra-virgin
    olive oil

- Warm the butter and oil in a large skillet over medium-high heat until the butter melts. Place the tuna in the skillet and cook for about 1 minute on each side. Do not overcook. Transfer the tuna to a cutting board, allow it to rest for 2 minutes, then cut it into quarter-inch slices. Serve the tuna on a bed of the salad.

> Pistachios are related to mangoes and sumac, a Middle Eastern spice.

The freshness of tuna comes through in a dish like poke, where the fish is accented with complementary and contrasting flavors and textures. Poke is a hallmark Hawaiian dish, and "onolicious" is island slang for delicious.

Because the tuna is served raw, look for the freshest in the market, and also look for sustainable seafood to ensure the continuation of the species.

ONOLICIOUS TUNA POKE LETTUCE CUPS

- In a large nonreactive bowl, whisk together the soy sauce, sesame oil, and olive oil. Stir in the scallions, onion, and pepper flakes. Add the tuna and toss to coat. Refrigerate, covered, until well chilled, but for no more than 2 hours.
- Spoon the tuna into each butter lettuce leaf, dividing it equally among the leaves. Garnish with the macadamia nuts, sesame seeds, and sea salt. Drizzle a bit of the remaining marinade over the tuna and a bit of the hot sauce around the plate. Serve immediately.

MAKES 4 TO 6 SERVINGS

½ cup soy sauce

2 tablespoons sesame oil

2 tablespoons extra-virgin olive oil

¾ cup finely chopped scallions, white and light green parts

¼ cup finely chopped sweet onion (such as Maui onion)

½ teaspoon red pepper flakes

2 pounds fresh tuna steak, cut into ¼-inch cubes

4 to 6 butter lettuce leaves (depending how many servings you are making)

2 tablespoons toasted, finely chopped macadamia nuts

½ tablespoon white sesame seeds

½ tablespoon black sesame seeds

2 teaspoons coarse sea salt

Asian hot sauce (such as sriracha), for drizzling

Two delicious Italian cheeses, fruity Parmigiano-Reggiano and sharp Romano, come together with pine nuts to form a zesty pesto. The result is a rich, fragrant sauce that adds a layer of herbaceous and nutty flavor to the flounder.

Store any leftover pesto in an airtight container in the refrigerator for three to four days. Try it on pasta, over sliced and toasted Italian bread, spooned on oysters, or as a dip for breadsticks.

PARMESAN-CRUSTED FLOUNDER WITH ZESTO PESTO

MAKES 4 SERVINGS

FOR THE PESTO:

2 cups basil leaves, torn

⅓ cup pine nuts

¼ cup freshly grated Parmigiano-Reggiano cheese

¼ cup freshly grated Romano cheese

3 cloves garlic, chopped

½ teaspoon kosher salt

½ teaspoon freshly ground black pepper

½ teaspoon crushed red pepper flakes

½ cup extra-virgin olive oil

- To make the pesto, in a food processor fitted with a steel blade attachment, pulse the basil and pine nuts until coarsely chopped. Add the cheeses and garlic, and pulse a few more times. Add the salt, pepper, and pepper flakes. With the blade running, slowly drizzle in the oil, stopping occasionally to scrape down the sides, until the mixture is mostly smooth.

- To prepare the fish, in a small bowl, combine the bread crumbs, cheese, oregano, and thyme. Spread the bread crumb mixture evenly on a plate. Dip the fish in the egg, then dredge both sides in the bread crumb mixture, evenly coating the fish.

- In a large sauté pan over medium heat, add enough oil to cover the bottom of the pan, and heat the oil to a low simmer. Carefully add the fillets; do not overcrowd the pan. Fry the fish for 4 to 5 minutes on each side, until the crust is golden and the flesh is flaky. Drain on paper towels and serve with pesto spooned on top.

FOR THE FISH:

½ cup bread crumbs

¼ cup freshly grated Parmigiano-Reggiano cheese

1 tablespoon fresh oregano leaves

1 tablespoon fresh thyme leaves

4 (½-pound) flounder fillets

1 egg, beaten

3 to 4 tablespoons extra-virgin olive oil

Scallops are one of the most delicate seafoods, and cooking them until they are just done is instrumental in making sure they don't turn into little rubbery hockey pucks. Their sweetness is accented here with citrus and earthy pistachios in a compound butter, served over large pasta noodles for fun.

PAN-SEARED SCALLOPS WITH ORANGE-PISTACHIO BUTTER OVER TAGLIATELLE PASTA

- To make the compound butter, in a small bowl, thoroughly combine the butter, pistachios, orange zest, salt, and pepper. Shape the butter into a log with wax paper, rolling it tightly, and refrigerate for at least 2 hours.
- To prepare the pasta and scallops, bring 4 quarts of salted water to a boil in a large stockpot over medium-high heat. Add the pasta and cook, stirring frequently, until it is al dente, 7 to 10 minutes. Drain and set aside.
- While the pasta cooks, wash the scallops under cold water, pat dry, and season both sides with the salt and pepper. In a medium skillet over high

(continued)

MAKES 4 TO 6 SERVINGS

FOR THE COMPOUND BUTTER:

¼ cup (½ stick) unsalted butter, softened

1 tablespoon pistachios, finely chopped

1 teaspoon orange zest

½ teaspoon kosher salt

¼ teaspoon freshly ground black pepper

FOR THE PASTA AND SCALLOPS:

½ pound dry tagliatelle pasta

16 dry-packed sea scallops

⅛ teaspoon kosher salt

⅛ teaspoon freshly ground black pepper

4 teaspoons peanut oil

1 small bunch flat-leaf parsley, roughly chopped

4 to 6 tablespoons pistachios, roughly chopped

heat, heat the oil. When it starts to smoke, add the scallops, cooking a few at a time so as not to crowd the pan. Sear the scallops until golden and a nice crust appears, 1 to 2 minutes. Turn the scallops and sear on the other side until golden, another 1 to 2 minutes.

- To serve, slice 4 to 6 half-inch-thick medallions from the compound butter. Arrange the scallops atop the pasta, place the butter medallions on top, and garnish with the parsley and pistachios.

Virginia is a major oyster-producing state, and the coastal waters are home to seven distinct growing regions, divided up based on geographical differences such as salinity and minerality. A nod to the Old Dominion, this recipe pairs Virginia oysters with other culinary calling cards from the state, including peanuts and country ham, to create a Rockefeller-style dish.

OYSTERS VIRGINIA

- In a food processor fitted with a steel blade attachment, pulse the arugula, parsley, peanuts, garlic, onions, Parmesan, lemon juice, sea salt, and pepper flakes until a coarse paste forms. Drizzle in the oil with the motor running. Transfer the mixture to a small bowl. Fold in the ham and set aside.
- Preheat the oven to 450 degrees F.
- Arrange the oysters in the shells on a large rimmed baking sheet, using piles of rock salt to steady them. Put a heaping teaspoon of the peanut mixture on each oyster and sprinkle with the bread crumbs. Bake the oysters until the bread crumbs start to become golden, 10 to 15 minutes. Top each oyster with a slice of cheese and bake until the cheese melts and browns, 1 to 2 minutes longer. Serve the oysters immediately with the lemon wedges.

1 cup arugula

½ cup flat-leaf parsley, finely chopped

¼ cup roasted, unsalted Virginia peanuts

3 cloves garlic, peeled

2 spring onions, white and green parts

2 tablespoons freshly grated Parmesan cheese

2 teaspoons freshly squeezed lemon juice

¼ teaspoon sea salt

¼ teaspoon red pepper flakes

½ cup extra-virgin olive oil

2 wafer-thin slices Virginia ham, finely chopped

24 oysters, shucked and shells reserved

Rock salt

¼ cup fine bread crumbs

24 thin (1-inch-square) slices firm or semifirm cheese

Lemon wedges, for serving

COOKIES

One of my cherished childhood memories was coming in through the kitchen door and smelling peanut butter cookies baking in the oven. My grandmother, known as Ma'am-Ma, made this recipe until she passed on Christmas, 2013, at age eighty-seven. Remembering folks we loved through their recipes keeps them alive in our hearts.

MA'AM-MA'S PEANUT BUTTER COOKIES

MAKES 3 DOZEN COOKIES

1 cup smooth Peanut Butter (page 27) or store-bought

1 cup sugar

1 egg

1 teaspoon baking soda

¼ cup all-purpose flour

- In a medium bowl, mix all the ingredients until thoroughly incorporated. Cover the bowl and refrigerate for 2 hours for the dough to firm.
- Preheat the oven to 325 degree F.
- With the palm of your hands, roll the dough into 1-inch balls and put them on an ungreased rimmed baking sheet a few inches apart. Lightly press down with the tines of a fork once, then again at a 90-degree angle, to form a crosshatch pattern; do not press too much—the cookie should retain its ball shape as much as possible.
- Bake until the cookies turn golden, 6 to 8 minutes. Cool them on the baking sheet for 15 minutes, then transfer to wire racks to cool completely. Store the cookies in an airtight container for 3 to 5 days.

> Arachibutyrophobia is the fear of getting peanut butter stuck to the roof of your mouth.

When I was growing up, a favorite dessert was pineapple upside-down cake, served hot from the cast-iron skillet in which it was made. Here, I've crafted those delicious flavors into a cookie, made even more indulgent with white chocolate chips.

PINEAPPLE UPSIDE-DOWN MACADAMIA COOKIES

- Preheat the oven to 350 degrees F.
- In a large bowl, beat the butter and sugars together until fluffy. Add the eggs and extracts and beat together.
- In a separate bowl, whisk together the flour, baking soda, and salt. Add the flour mixture slowly to the wet ingredients, about ½ cup at a time, stirring and mixing well. Add the chocolate chips, nuts, pineapple, and cherries, and mix until thoroughly incorporated.
- Scoop the dough in rounded tablespoonfuls and put them on an ungreased rimmed baking sheet a few inches apart. Bake until the cookies spread out and turn golden brown, 8 to 12 minutes. Cool them on the baking sheet for about 5 minutes, then transfer to wire racks to cool completely. Store the cookies in an airtight container for 3 to 5 days.

MAKES ABOUT 4½ DOZEN COOKIES

1 cup (2 sticks) unsalted butter, softened

1 cup packed dark brown sugar

½ cup granulated sugar

2 eggs

½ teaspoon vanilla extract

½ teaspoon orange extract or orange liqueur

2¼ cups all-purpose flour

1 teaspoon baking soda

1 teaspoon kosher salt

2 cups white chocolate chips

1 cup chopped macadamia nuts

½ cup finely chopped candied pineapple

½ cup chopped dried cherries

The macadamia nut was named by botanist Ferdinand von Mueller in honor of his friend, the chemist, medical teacher, and politician John Macadam, in 1857.

Light and airy, these meringues are heavenly with a quick dip in melted white chocolate and a rolling in finely chopped almonds. Enjoy them plain, crumbled atop a big bowl of ice cream, or layered in trifles.

ALMOND MERINGUE KISSES

MAKES 12 TO 16 COOKIES

4 large egg whites

⅔ cup granulated sugar

¾ cup confectioners' sugar

1 cup white chocolate chips

1 cup toasted almonds, finely chopped

- Preheat the oven to 200 degrees F. Line a rimmed baking sheet with parchment paper.
- In a large bowl, using an electric mixer, beat the egg whites until frothy, about 1 minute. With the mixer running, slowly add in the granulated sugar and beat until medium peaks form, 8 to 10 minutes. With the mixer still running, slowly add in the confectioners' sugar and beat until stiff peaks form, an additional 4 to 6 minutes.
- By the heaping tablespoonful, mound meringues on the prepared baking sheet and bake until dry, 2 to 2½ hours. Turn off the heat and let the meringues remain in the oven for an additional hour, or until cool.
- Using a double boiler, melt the chocolate chips. For instructions on how to melt chocolate in a double boiler or how to create your own double boiler, see Using a Double Boiler (page 41).

- To assemble the meringues, line a rimmed baking sheet with parchment paper. Spread the almonds evenly on a large plate. Dip the bottom of each meringue into the chocolate, shake carefully to remove any excess, then dip it into the almonds, pressing gently to make sure they adhere. Shake carefully to remove excess almonds. Place the meringues on the prepared baking sheet and let them sit for about 30 minutes to set. Store the cookies in an airtight container for 3 to 5 days

Almonds are ground into a paste to create marzipan, which is molded into fruit or other shapes, realistically painted with edible coloring, and sold as holiday treats.

Popular for centuries, jumbles are a time-honored cookie-like pastry with a long history in the South. A popular baked good with travelers, they may have made their way on ocean passages between England and Virginia in the late seventeenth and early eighteenth centuries, becoming part of the American diet. Martha Washington has directions for them in her Booke of Cookery recipe collection.

MARTHA WASHINGTON JUMBLE COOKIES

- Preheat the oven to 350 degrees F.
- In a medium bowl, beat the butter and sugars together until light and fluffy. Add the egg and beat to incorporate. Sift the flour, baking soda, cinnamon, nutmeg, and cayenne into the mixture and stir to combine. Fold in the raisins and pecans, and mix well.
- Drop the dough in heaping tablespoonfuls on a rimmed baking sheet approximately 2 inches apart; do not crowd the cookies. Bake until the cookies are lightly browned, 12 to 14 minutes. Transfer the cookies to wire racks to cool completely and repeat with the remaining dough.
- To make the glaze, in a large bowl whisk together the sugar, vanilla, and 2 tablespoons of the cream until smooth. Add the additional tablespoon of cream if needed to thin the glaze.
- Drizzle the glaze over the cooled cookies. Store the cookies in an airtight container for 3 to 5 days or in the freezer for up to 6 months.

MAKES 6 TO 8 DOZEN COOKIES

FOR THE COOKIES:

½ cup (1 stick) unsalted butter, softened

½ cup granulated sugar

¼ cup packed light brown sugar

1 egg

1¼ cups flour

½ teaspoon baking soda

¼ teaspoon ground cinnamon

¼ teaspoon freshly grated nutmeg

⅛ teaspoon cayenne pepper

1 cup golden raisins

1 cup chopped pecans

FOR THE GLAZE:

1 cup confectioners' sugar

½ teaspoon vanilla extract

2 to 3 tablespoons heavy cream

OTHER
SWEETS

Brownies are generally craved by most, but the more decadent, the better. The chocolate chips on the top melt into ooey-gooey goodness: the perfect foil to the salty walnuts. To make them extra sinful, top the warm brownies with vanilla ice cream and drizzle them with Hazelnut-Bourbon-Chocolate Sauce (page 29).

COMATOSE BY CHOCOLATE BROWNIES

- Preheat the oven to 350 degrees F. Grease a 13-by-9-inch baking pan.
- In a large bowl, whisk together the sugar, flour, cocoa, baking powder, and salt. In a medium bowl, beat the eggs, oil, and extracts just until incorporated.
- Make a well in the dry ingredients and fold in the wet ingredients completely. Fold in ½ cup of the walnuts and the chocolate chips. Pour the batter into the prepared pan, spreading it out and smoothing it with a spatula. Evenly sprinkle on the remaining 1 cup walnuts, pressing them slightly into the batter with the spatula.
- Bake until the brownies slightly rise, the walnuts are turning golden, and a toothpick inserted in the center comes out clean, 23 to 25 minutes. Cool the brownies in the pan, then cut them into pieces approximately 2¼ inches by 3¼ inches.

MAKES 16 BROWNIES

2 cups sugar

1⅓ cups all-purpose flour

¾ cup unsweetened cocoa powder

1 teaspoon baking powder

½ teaspoon kosher salt

4 eggs

⅔ cup canola oil

1½ teaspoons vanilla extract

½ teaspoon almond extract

1½ cups walnuts, divided

½ cup semisweet chocolate chips

For years people have been fans of s'mores: the classic combination of chocolate, marshmallow, and graham crackers. They are staples for outdoor fun. This version has even more to love when you swap the traditional milk chocolate bar for walnut-infused chocolate bark, and baking them in the oven makes them a year-round treat.

CHOCOLATE WALNUT BARK S'MORES

MAKES 4 SERVINGS

FOR THE BARK:

1 cup milk chocolate chips

1 cup toasted walnuts, chopped

FOR THE S'MORES:

8 graham cracker squares

4 marshmallows

- To make the bark, very lightly grease a rimmed baking sheet or line it with parchment paper.
- Using a double boiler, melt the chocolate chips. For instructions on how to melt chocolate in a double boiler or how to create your own double boiler, see Using a Double Boiler (page 41).
- Quickly and carefully pour the melted chocolate onto the prepared baking sheet and spread it out with the spatula into a 7-inch square that is about ¼ inch thick. Evenly distribute the walnut pieces across the chocolate, using the spatula to carefully push them into the chocolate to ensure they adhere. Freeze the bark, uncovered, until firm, about 20 minutes.
- Remove the bark from the freezer and allow it to just come to room temperature. Using a serrated knife, cut it into four 3½-inch square pieces.
- To make the s'mores, preheat the oven to 400 degrees F.

- Break or trim the graham crackers to 4½-inch squares and place 4 on a baking sheet. Top each with a piece of chocolate walnut bark. Using kitchen scissors, trim ⅛ inch off the end of each marshmallow. Discard (or eat) the ends and place the marshmallows, trimmed side down, on top of each piece of chocolate bark. (By removing just a bit of the marshmallow, the uncoated, sticky side adheres to the chocolate and prevents the marshmallow from tipping over.)
- Bake the s'mores until the marshmallow puffs and begins to toast, 3 to 5 minutes. Remove them from the oven and press the remaining graham crackers on top to form a sandwich. Serve immediately.

More than 99 percent of all the walnuts in the United States are grown in California's Central Valley.

Bask in the homey flavors of this dense, rich cake filled with spices, chopped apples, and lots of earthy hazelnuts, made just a tad sweeter with a simple glaze drizzled on top. Inspired by a recipe from the Virginia State Apple Board, it's great served at breakfast or brunch (try toasting a slice) or for dessert. It also makes an incredible bread pudding or French toast. For a salty-sweet twist, try sprinkling coarse sea salt on top of the glaze before slicing.

HAZELNUT-APPLE CAKE WITH BOURBON GLAZE

MAKES 8 TO 10 SERVINGS

FOR THE CAKE:

3 cups all-purpose flour

1 cup granulated sugar

1 cup packed light brown sugar

2 teaspoons baking soda

2 teaspoons ground cinnamon

1 teaspoon kosher salt

1 teaspoon ground allspice

½ teaspoon ground ginger

2 eggs

- To make the cake, preheat the oven to 350 degrees F. Grease a standard tube or Bundt pan and set aside.
- In a large mixing bowl, whisk together the flour, sugars, baking soda, cinnamon, salt, allspice, and ginger. Make a well in the center and add the eggs, applesauce, and oil; stir to incorporate. Fold in the apples, hazelnuts, and lemon juice; the batter will be stiff. Scrape the batter into the prepared pan and bake until the top is golden and a toothpick inserted in the cake comes out clean, about 1 hour.

- Cool the cake in the pan for 10 minutes, then invert onto a wire rack to cool completely.
- While the cake cools, make the glaze. In a medium saucepan over medium-high heat, add the bourbon, sugars, and butter; bring to a boil and stir occasionally until the sugars dissolve.
- Cut slits around the top of the cake and slowly pour the glaze over, allowing time for it to absorb a bit in between drizzles.

½ cup applesauce

½ cup vegetable oil

4½ cups finely chopped peeled apples

1 cup toasted hazelnuts, chopped

2 tablespoons freshly squeezed lemon juice

FOR THE GLAZE:

1 cup bourbon

2 tablespoons packed light brown sugar

2 tablespoons confectioners' sugar

1 tablespoon unsalted butter

A traditional party favorite gets kicked up a notch with the addition of rich, buttery macadamia nuts. Quick and easy to prepare, these are also great to give as gifts when put in a pretty box.

MACADAMIA CHOCOLATE RUM BALLS

- In a large bowl, combine the vanilla wafer crumbs, 1 cup of the sugar, the nuts, and cocoa powder. In a small bowl, whisk together the corn syrup and rum. Pour the rum mixture over the vanilla wafer mixture, and stir well to completely incorporate. Refrigerate the mixture for 5 minutes.
- Place the remaining ¾ cup sugar in a large bowl. Scoop the wafer mixture into 1-inch balls (the larger end of a melon baller is just the right size) and roll them in the sugar.
- Transfer the balls to an airtight container and refrigerate for at least 1 day or up to 3 weeks before serving to allow the flavors to meld. Roll in additional sugar before serving.

MAKES ABOUT 4 DOZEN RUM BALLS

1 (12-ounce) box vanilla wafers, crumbled

1¾ cups confectioners' sugar, divided

1 cup chopped, toasted macadamia nuts

2 tablespoons unsweetened cocoa powder

2½ tablespoons light corn syrup

½ cup dark rum

Europeans discovered the macadamia in Australia in 1828; the first commercial orchard was planted there in the 1880s and in Hawaii in the 1920s.

Chocolate bark is a longtime favorite. This recipe comes together with a few simple ingredients and steps, but looks and tastes like the store-bought candy, at a fraction of the cost.

CHOCOLATE-COVERED DRIED CHERRY & CASHEW BARK

MAKES 8 PIECES

1 cup milk chocolate chips

1 cup semisweet chocolate chips

1 cup toasted cashews, chopped

1 cup fresh dark cherries, pitted and chopped

1 cup white chocolate chips

- Very lightly grease 2 rimmed baking sheets or line them with parchment paper, and set them aside.

- Using a double boiler, melt the chocolate chips. For instructions on how to melt chocolate in a double boiler or how to create your own double boiler, see Using a Double Boiler (page 41).

- Quickly and carefully pour the melted chocolate onto the prepared baking sheets and spread it out with the spatula on each sheet into a 7-inch square about ¼ inch thick. Evenly distribute the cashew and cherry pieces across the chocolate, using the spatula to carefully push them into the chocolate to ensure they adhere.

- Melt the white chocolate chips using the same method. When the chocolate has melted, dip the tines of a fork into the chocolate, then drizzle it over the prepared bark for garnish.

- Freeze the bark, uncovered, until firm, about 20 minutes. Remove the bark from the freezer and allow it to just come to room temperature. Using a serrated knife, cut it into 3½-inch square pieces.

Perhaps the only thing better than fresh fruit is grilled fresh fruit. Here, ripe, juicy apricots, which have complementary flavors to almonds, are pan-seared to bring out their natural sugars and topped with creamy, nut-infused mascarpone cheese.

GRILLED APRICOTS WITH BROWN SUGAR–ALMOND MASCARPONE

- To make the mascarpone, in a medium bowl using an electric mixer, beat the cheese, cream, sugar, and cinnamon until smooth and completely combined. Fold in the almonds and set aside.
- To prepare the apricots, brush the halves on all sides with the oil. In a grill pan over medium heat, place the apricots, cut side down, and grill undisturbed until grill marks form and the apricots are slightly softened and heated, 5 to 7 minutes. Flip the apricots and grill for another 2 to 3 minutes.
- To serve, place 2 apricots on each plate, cut side up. Drizzle the almond liqueur over the apricots and spoon mascarpone cheese in each indentation. Garnish with the chopped almonds and thyme sprigs.

> Some 80 percent of the world's almonds are produced in California.

MAKES 4 SERVINGS

FOR THE MASCARPONE:

8 ounces mascarpone cheese, at room temperature

1 tablespoon heavy cream

¼ cup packed light brown sugar

1 teaspoon ground cinnamon

¼ cup toasted almonds, chopped

FOR THE APRICOTS:

4 apricots, halved and pitted

¼ cup canola oil

4 teaspoons almond liqueur

FOR GARNISH:

¼ cup toasted almonds, chopped

Fresh thyme sprigs

At a New Orleans cooking class several years back, we made several versions of bread pudding, each of the offerings as good as the next. Inspired by that trip, here is my recipe, made decadent with the addition of a little rum, a pecan crumble, and a sinfully sweet sauce to pour on top.

NEW ORLEANS BREAD PUDDING WITH PECAN CRUMBLE & RUM SAUCE

- To make the crumble, in a medium bowl, cream the sugar and butter. Fold in the pecans until they are coated with the mixture. Set the crumble aside.
- To make the pudding, preheat the oven to 350 degrees F. Grease a 9-by-13-inch baking dish and set it aside.
- In a large bowl, whisk together the egg yolks, cream, sugar, cinnamon, vanilla, and rum. Add the bread cubes and toss to coat completely. Pour the mixture into the prepared baking dish and let it sit for about 30 minutes for the bread to absorb the liquid. Sprinkle the crumble mixture evenly on top and bake until golden, 50 to 60 minutes. The pudding should be firm and set, but moist.

(continued)

MAKES 6 TO 8 SERVINGS

FOR THE CRUMBLE:

½ cup packed light brown sugar

¼ cup (½ stick) unsalted butter, softened

1 cup pecans, chopped

FOR THE BREAD PUDDING:

5 egg yolks

2 cups heavy cream

6 tablespoons dark brown sugar

1 teaspoon ground cinnamon

1 teaspoon vanilla extract

1 teaspoon dark rum

6 to 7 cups French bread, cut into ½-inch cubes

FOR THE SAUCE:

⅓ cup heavy cream

½ cup (1 stick) unsalted butter

1 cup packed light brown sugar

1½ tablespoons dark rum

- To make the sauce, in a heavy saucepan over medium-low heat, add the cream and butter and stir until the butter melts, about 1 to 2 minutes. Add the sugar and stir until the sugar dissolves, about 2 to 3 minutes. Reduce the heat to low and add the rum, stirring to incorporate. Pour the sauce over the pudding and serve hot or cold.

Pecans are native to the southern United States as well as Mexico. The name comes from an Algonquian word that means "nuts requiring a stone to crack."

A favorite flavor combination of mine is chocolate, coffee, and orange. There is something very simple but oh-so-sophisticated when those elements come together, as they do in this recipe. Rolling the truffles in finely chopped pistachios takes them over the top. Enjoy these as a treat, or make a batch to give as gifts.

MOCHA VALENCIA TRUFFLES

- In a heavy saucepan over medium heat, bring the cream to a gentle, rolling boil, then remove the pan from the heat. Put the chocolate chips in a stainless steel or glass bowl and pour the hot cream over top. Add the liqueurs and orange zest. Let the mixture sit for 5 minutes, then stir it until smooth. Cool the mixture at room temperature, then cover the bowl and refrigerate for 2 hours. Line a rimmed baking sheet with parchment paper and set it aside.

- Form truffles with a melon baller or teaspoon, and quickly roll them in your hand. Place them on the prepared baking sheet, cover the sheet with plastic wrap, and refrigerate overnight.

- The next day, roll the truffles in the pistachios. Store them in an airtight container in the refrigerator for 3 to 5 days.

MAKES 8 TO 10 TRUFFLES

1 cup heavy cream

2 cups semisweet chocolate chips

1 teaspoon orange liqueur or extract

1 teaspoon coffee liqueur

1 teaspoon orange zest

1 cup pistachios, finely chopped

A few years ago a friend shared some delicious banana ice cream, as well as a secret: it was made with one ingredient: the banana alone. The results are quick, easy, and healthy. Here is a rendition with a few more goodies thrown in to complement the banana and satisfy your sweet tooth.

BANANA-CASHEW-GINGER FREEZER ICE CREAM

- Line a rimmed baking sheet with parchment paper. Lay the banana slices on the sheet, cover the sheet with plastic wrap, and freeze until completely frozen, about 3 hours.

- In a food processor fitted with a steel blade attachment, pulse to break the banana slices them up. Add 1 tablespoon of the condensed milk. Blend until the bananas reach a smooth, creamy consistency, like soft-serve ice cream, about 3 to 5 minutes. Add the remaining 1 tablespoon condensed milk, the vanilla, ginger, and cashew butter and pulse to blend. Transfer to a freezer container, fold in the chopped cashews, and freeze until solid, about 5 hours.

MAKES 2 SERVINGS

1 cup (½-inch) banana slices (from 2 to 3 ripe bananas)

2 tablespoons sweetened condensed milk, divided

½ teaspoon vanilla extract

½ teaspoon ground ginger

3 tablespoons homemade cashew butter (see Peanut Butter recipe, page 27) or store-bought

¼ cup chopped cashews

The cashew is largely grown in Brazil, India, and certain East African nations, and is always sold already shelled because the casing around the nut is toxic.

Wonderful as a breakfast or brunch dish, or as a dessert to cap off a Southern-themed dinner, this offering is a study of complementary flavors. The earthy, naturally sweet flavors of sweet potatoes and pecans are accented with luscious fried apples and a sweet compound butter of maple syrup and ground cinnamon.

FRIED APPLES ON SWEET POTATO–PECAN BISCUITS WITH MAPLE-CINNAMON BUTTER

MAKES 10 TO 12 SERVINGS

FOR THE COMPOUND BUTTER:

1 cup (2 sticks) unsalted butter, softened

½ cup maple syrup

2 teaspoons ground cinnamon

FOR THE BISCUITS:

2 cups all-purpose flour

½ cup sugar

2½ teaspoons baking powder

1½ teaspoons kosher salt

¼ teaspoon ground cinnamon

¼ teaspoon ground nutmeg

½ cup vegetable shortening

- To make the compound butter, in a medium bowl using an electric mixer, whip the butter with the maple syrup and cinnamon until the butter is fluffy and the mixture is well blended. Set the butter aside.
- To make the biscuits, preheat the oven to 425 degrees F. Grease a rimmed baking sheet and set it aside.
- In a medium bowl, whisk together the flour, sugar, baking powder, salt, cinnamon, and nutmeg. Work the shortening into the flour mixture with a pastry cutter until well mixed. Fold in the sweet potatoes, add the pecans, and knead, adding a little more flour if the dough is too wet. If the dough is too dry, add the milk a little at a time. The mixture should be firm and smooth.

- Roll out the dough on a floured cutting board to about ½-inch thickness and use a biscuit cutter to form biscuits. Place the biscuits on the prepared baking sheet and brush the melted butter on top. Bake until the tops are light brown, about 15 minutes; reduce the heat to 400 degrees F if the tops are cooking too quickly.
- To prepare the apples, peel, core, and cut the apples into ¼-inch wedges. In a medium bowl, toss the apples in the lemon juice and set them aside.
- In a sauté pan over medium heat, melt the butter. Add the sugar, cinnamon, ginger, and salt and stir. Add the apples and cook, stirring occasionally, until they soften and are fork-tender but not mushy, 5 to 8 minutes.
- To serve, split open the biscuits, spread them with the compound butter, and spoon on the apples. Garnish with the pecans.

2 cups peeled sweet potatoes, baked and mashed (about 4 medium potatoes)

1 cup toasted pecans, finely chopped

2 to 4 tablespoons whole milk

¼ cup (½ stick) unsalted butter, melted

FOR THE APPLES:

8 Granny Smith apples

3 to 4 tablespoons freshly squeezed lemon juice (from 2 medium lemons)

1 cup (2 sticks) unsalted butter

1 cup packed dark brown sugar

1 tablespoon ground cinnamon

2 teaspoons ground ginger

1 teaspoon kosher salt

FOR GARNISH:

1 cup Candied Pecans (page 39), chopped

Peanut brittle is one of those confections that conjures up childhood happiness. The subtle flavor of the pine nuts, encased in shards of caramelized sugar, is made even more delightful thanks to the melted dark chocolate and a sprinkling of sea salt.

DARK CHOCOLATE PINE NUT BRITTLE

- To make the brittle, line a rimmed baking sheet with parchment paper and set it aside.
- In a heavy-bottomed saucepan over medium-high heat, add the sugar and cook, stirring with a wooden spoon, until the sugar melts and becomes golden in color. Add the pine nuts and stir; add the butter and stir. Keep stirring until the butter melts and the mixture is well incorporated. Stir in the salt.
- Pour the mixture onto the prepared baking sheet, using the back of the spoon to evenly spread it out so it is about ¼ inch thick. Allow to cool completely, about 1 hour, then break into about 2-inch pieces.
- To make the chocolate, line a rimmed baking sheet with parchment paper and set it aside. Place the salt in a small bowl.
- Using a double boiler, melt the chocolate chips. For instructions on how to melt chocolate in a double boiler or how to create your own double boiler, see Using a Double Boiler (page 41).
- Dip half of each piece of brittle in the melted chocolate, shaking gently to remove any excess, and dip again. Place the dipped brittle on the prepared baking sheet, smooth side down, and, while the chocolate is still wet, sprinkle it with a bit of sea salt.

MAKES ABOUT 2 DOZEN PIECES

FOR THE BRITTLE:

2 cups sugar

2½ cups pine nuts

½ cup (1 stick) unsalted butter

½ teaspoon kosher salt

FOR THE CHOCOLATE:

Sea salt, for sprinkling

1 cup dark chocolate chips

This sinfully good chestnut puree, sweetened with simple syrup and a bit of quality vanilla extract, is a perfect complement to the complex flavors of a ripe, grilled pear. The puree also makes a wonderful topping on cupcakes, filling in crepes, or stand-alone treat to eat by the spoonful.

PAN-SEARED PEARS STUFFED WITH CHESTNUT PUREE

MAKES 4 SERVINGS

FOR THE PUREE:

1 cup sugar

2 cups water

1½ pounds roasted or boiled chestnuts, shelled and halved

1 teaspoons vanilla extract

FOR THE PEARS:

4 pears, halved

¼ cup extra-virgin olive oil

2 teaspoons sea salt

- To make the puree, in a heavy saucepan over medium heat, bring the sugar and water to a boil, stirring constantly. Add the chestnuts and stir until the sugar has completely dissolved and mixture is syrupy, about 5 to 7 minutes. Set aside.
- Using a colander or sieve over a medium bowl, drain the chestnuts, reserving the syrup. In a food processor fitted with a steel blade attachment, pulse the chestnuts, 2 to 3 tablespoons of the reserved syrup, and the vanilla. Pulse, adding additional syrup a few teaspoons at a time if necessary, until the puree is smooth, about 4 to 6 minutes, scraping down the sides of the bowl as needed.

- To prepare the pears, using a melon baller, scoop out the core of each pear half and brush on all sides with the oil. In a grill pan over medium heat, place the pears, cut side down, and grill, undisturbed, until grill marks form and the pears are slightly softened and heated, 8 to 10 minutes. Flip the pears and grill for another 3 to 4 minutes.
- To serve, place 2 pears on each plate, cut side up, sprinkle with the sea salt, and spoon the puree in each indentation. Serve immediately. Store any remaining chestnut puree in an airtight container in the refrigerator for up to 5 days.

Chocolate and hazelnuts have a true affinity; just ask Pietro Ferrero, who invented Nutella. This cocktail turns that delicious combination into a great cocktail to enjoy when relaxing or in lieu of dessert—or, let's face it, in addition to dessert.

NUTTY FELLA MARTINI

- To make the rim, in a small bowl, combine the chocolate and hazelnuts. Transfer them to a small plate. Pour the chocolate syrup on another small plate. Invert a chilled martini glass and dip it into the chocolate syrup, allowing the excess to drip off, then dip it into the hazelnut mixture, rotating the glass to completely coat the rim.
- To make the cocktail, fill a cocktail shaker with ice. Add the vodka, liqueurs, and almond milk, cover, and shake. Strain into the prepared martini glass.

Oregon is a large producer of hazelnuts, which became its official state nut in 1989.

MAKES 1 COCKTAIL

FOR THE RIM:

1 ounce milk chocolate, finely grated

2 to 3 toasted hazelnuts, finely chopped

1 to 2 ounces chocolate syrup

FOR THE COCKTAIL:

1 ounce vodka

1 ounce hazelnut liqueur (such as Frangelico)

½ ounce dark crème de cacao

1 ounce Almond Milk (page 31) or store-bought

CONVERSIONS

VOLUME			LENGTH		WEIGHT	
UNITED STATES	METRIC	IMPERIAL	UNITED STATES	METRIC	AVOIRDUPOIS	METRIC
¼ tsp.	1.25 ml		⅛ in.	3 mm	¼ oz.	7 g
½ tsp.	2.5 ml		¼ in.	6 mm	½ oz.	15 g
1 tsp.	5 ml		½ in.	1.25 cm	1 oz.	30 g
½ Tbsp.	7.5 ml		1 in.	2.5 cm	2 oz.	60 g
1 Tbsp.	15 ml		1 ft.	30 cm	3 oz.	90 g
⅛ c.	30 ml	1 fl. oz.			4 oz.	115 g
¼ c.	60 ml	2 fl. oz.			5 oz.	150 g
⅓ c.	80 ml	2.5 fl. oz.			6 oz.	175 g
½ c.	125 ml	4 fl. oz.			7 oz.	200 g
1 c.	250 ml	8 fl. oz.			8 oz. (½ lb.)	225 g
2 c. (1 pt.)	500 ml	16 fl. oz.			9 oz.	250 g
1 qt.	1 l	32 fl. oz.			10 oz.	300 g

TEMPERATURE				WEIGHT (cont.)	
				11 oz.	325 g
OVEN MARK	FAHRENHEIT	CELSIUS	GAS	12 oz.	350 g
Very cool	250–275	130–140	½–1	13 oz.	375 g
Cool	300	150	2	14 oz.	400 g
Warm	325	165	3	15 oz.	425 g
Moderate	350	175	4	16 oz. (1 lb.)	450 g
Moderately hot	375	190	5	1½ lb.	750 g
	400	200	6	2 lb.	900 g
Hot	425	220	7	2¼ lb.	1 kg
	450	230	8	3 lb.	1.4 kg
Very Hot	475	245	9	4 lb.	1.8 kg

INDEX

NOTE: Photographs are indicated by *italics*.

ABOUT THE AUTHOR

PATRICK EVANS-HYLTON is an award-winning food journalist based in Norfolk, VA.

Trained as a chef at Johnson & Wales University, Evans-Hylton has covered food and foodways through print, radio, television, and social media since 1995.

He is author of two food history books and three cookbooks, teaches a number of food writing classes, is the founder of the Mid-Atlantic Food Writers Symposium, and runs a cooking and wine school at Taste Unlimited, an area gourmet grocer.

Evans-Hylton serves on many boards and is an active volunteer with such groups as the Virginia Aquarium's Sensible Seafood Program and Culinary Institute of Virginia. He is also a member of the International Association of Culinary Professionals.

He is a James Beard Foundation media awards judge and a culinary advisor to the commonwealth of Virginia.

Evans-Hylton blogs at PatrickEvansHylton.com.